THE IDEA OF
PRISON ABOLITION

CARL G. HEMPEL LECTURE SERIES

THE IDEA OF PRISON ABOLITION

TOMMIE SHELBY

PRINCETON UNIVERSITY PRESS

PRINCETON AND OXFORD

Published by Princeton University Press
41 William Street, Princeton, New Jersey 08540
99 Banbury Road, Oxford OX2 6JX

press.princeton.edu

All Rights Reserved

First paperback printing, 2024
Paperback ISBN 978-0-691-22976-8
Cloth ISBN 978-0-691-22975-1
ISBN (e-book) 978-0-691-22977-5

British Library Cataloging-in-Publication Data is available

Editorial: Matt Rohal
Production Editorial: Ellen Foos
Cover image: Sonny Mauricio / Unsplash; delray77 / iStock
Cover design by Ben Higgins
Production: Erin Suydam
Publicity: Kate Hensley and Carmen Jimenez
Copyeditor: Jodi Beder

This book has been composed in Arno Pro with Futura display

Printed in the United States of America

In memory of my beloved grandmother, Mattie Brock

CONTENTS

ACKNOWLEDGMENTS

In *Dark Ghettos* (2016), I argued that black metropolitan neighborhoods with high levels of concentrated disadvantage should, on grounds of justice, be abolished. Ending ghettoization would, I said, require a radical transformation of the basic structure of U.S. society, and I insisted that such efforts at fundamental change should include the ghetto poor as essential and equal partners. This book asks whether prisons, which incarcerate an extraordinary number of ghetto denizens, should also be abolished.

The Idea of Prison Abolition began as the Carl G. Hempel Lectures, which I delivered at Princeton University in 2018. I am immensely grateful for the Princeton Philosophy Department's invitation and for its warm hospitality. I received invaluable critical feedback on the project during my campus visit, and I thoroughly enjoyed, and learned from, the many conversations, formal and informal, that my lectures provoked. I was able to devote myself to writing these lectures, with time away from my regular academic responsibilities, because of a generous fellowship from the Andrew Carnegie Foundation.

An earlier version of Chapter 1 appeared as "Army of the Wronged: Autobiography, Political Prisoners, and Black

Radicalism," in *Cannons and Codes: Law, Literature, and America's Wars*, ed. Alison LaCroix, Jonathan Masur, Martha Nussbaum, and Laura Weinrib (Oxford University Press, 2021). Chapter 4 is a revised version of "What's Wrong with the Prison Industrial Complex? Profit, Privatization, and the Circumstances of Injustice," in *A Political Economy of Justice*, ed. Danielle Allen, Yochai Benkler, Leah Downey, Rebecca Henderson, and Josh Simons (University of Chicago Press, 2022).

As with my previous monographs, this book combines my interests in philosophy and black studies. My devotion to these two academic fields has been nurtured and strengthened by colleagues and students in the Department of African and African American Studies and the Department of Philosophy at Harvard University. I owe a special thanks to the students in my "Punishment and Imprisonment" seminar. It was enormously helpful to think through these ideas with you. The students and faculty in my colleague Lucas Stanczyk's "State Violence" seminar also provided useful critical feedback on several chapters. And I'm grateful to the participants in my colleague Brandon Terry's "Philosophy, Social Thought, and Criticism" workshop for their critical engagement with material from the manuscript.

Elizabeth Hinton, Christopher Lewis, Lucas Stanczyk, Brandon Terry, and Adaner Usmani read drafts of the manuscript and offered many useful suggestions and constructive criticisms. Many other colleagues, students, and friends offered helpful feedback on chapter drafts or provided other advice and valuable assistance, including Danielle Allen, Richard Arneson, Lawrie Balfour, David Brink, Bruno Carvalho, Paul Clarke, Ruth Coffey, Derrick Darby, Janine de Novais, Candice Delmas, Justin Driver, Lidal Dror, Tweedy Flanigan, Thomas Frampton, Lori

Gruen, Deborah Hellman, David Jenkins, Corey Katz, Erin Kelly, Randall Kennedy, David Knight, Issa Kohler-Hausmann, Christopher Kutz, Rose Lenehan, Mohan Matthen, Tracey Meares, Christia Mercer, Darrel Moellendorf, Osagie Obasogie, Deborah Poritz, Gurpreet Rattan, Judith Resnik, Luke Roelofs, Wendy Salkin, Robert Sampson, Tim Scanlon, Seana Shiffrin, Kaia Stern, Iakovos Vasiliou, Jeremy Waldron, James Whitman, and Leo Zaibert.

Over the last few years, I have presented ideas and arguments from the book project as lectures, conference talks, and workshop papers at several universities, including Brandeis University, CUNY Graduate Center, Harvard University, Humboldt University of Berlin, Goethe University, Leiden University, London School of Economics, Loyola University in Chicago, New York University, Oxford University, Saint Louis University, Stanford University, Tufts University, UC Berkeley, UC San Diego, University College London, University of Copenhagen, University of North Carolina at Chapel Hill, University of Pittsburgh, University of Toronto, University of Virginia, University of Warwick, University of Wisconsin, and Yale University. I'm grateful for the invitations to present my work in progress and for the feedback and suggestions from participants at those events.

The book has been improved because of the thoughtful and sometimes sharply critical comments from three anonymous reviewers for Princeton University Press. I did not follow their advice in every instance, but I benefited greatly from giving every suggestion serious consideration. Matt Rohal, my extraordinary editor, went far beyond the call of duty. He not only provided extensive feedback on every chapter but pushed me to make the book better using a perfect balance of constructive criticism, patience, and encouragement. I also thank Rob Tempio, Publisher at Princeton University Press, for his professionalism and guidance throughout the process. Jodi Beder is a meticulous, thoughtful, and efficient copy editor. Ellen Foos kept the production trains running on time. I thank David Luljak for composing the index and Kierstan Kaushal-Carter for assisting with proofreading. I am grateful for the assistance of Wendy Salkin, Sarah Brophy, and Julian Davis in writing the discussion questions for the paperback edition. Bréond Durr was an invaluable and resourceful research assistant, and I look forward to seeing him soon make his mark rethinking juvenile imprisonment.

I also want to thank Angela Davis, whom I have long admired, for her extraordinary writings and steadfast commitment to fighting for the freedom of the oppressed. It was reflecting on her life and work that stirred me to think through the role of prisons in modern society.

Although my wife Jessie knows the depths of my debts to her, I want to thank her here, once again, for her steady loving support, patient ear, and wise editorial hand. I'm deeply grateful to my kids Ella and Christopher for their good will and tolerance as I wrote another "boring" book instead of spending more time with them. I dedicate this book to the memory of my grandmother Mattie Brock, who saved her adolescent grandson from falling into the abyss when he had lost his way.

Introduction: Reform or Abolition?

The United States has a higher imprisonment rate than any country on the planet, with more than twenty-five percent of the world's prisoners.[1] Walnut Street Prison, the first in the nation, opened in Philadelphia in 1773, initially as a conventional jail and then expanded in 1790 into a state penitentiary, where convicted prisoners were required to perform hard labor in solitude.[2] But forms of incarceration, used for a variety of purposes, have existed in other places for centuries. While many historical examples are obviously horrifying and inhumane, today's prisons, in the United States and elsewhere, continue to raise serious questions of justice and human rights.

It is a hopeful sign of moral progress that many believe prison systems, around the globe but especially in the United States, are in urgent need of fundamental change. The problem of mass incarceration has received broad and deep news coverage. Numerous public stories, both reported and first-person accounts, detail the generally dreadful lives of prisoners. Persistent and sometimes militant activism is directed at reforming prisons, jails, and immigration detention centers. What is more, the belief that major reforms are needed in our prisons, and in our criminal law systems more broadly, cuts across the political spectrum, with many conservatives joining the call.[3]

More recently, a growing number of voices call for more than reform. They demand that we stop using prisons altogether. This political and philosophical outlook—known as "prison abolition" or sometimes "penal abolition"—rejects the very idea that incarceration can be a justified penalty for committing a crime. Prison abolition is radical, counterintuitive, and strikes some as absurd. But perhaps the abolitionists are correct—that prisons simply cannot be reformed, that even the most ideal prison would be indefensible. Prisons do tremendous and lasting harm, and this damage extends beyond prisoners to their families and communities. If a society relies on prisons, as all modern societies do, this use demands compelling defense. And so I welcome the call to scrutinize this longstanding practice.

Those convinced that prison reform is feasible and required by justice have long argued against defenders of the status quo and against those who benefit from the current broken system. Yet, with rising interest in and advocacy for prison abolition, it has now become essential for advocates of prison reform to put their views on trial against a significant and potentially superior alternative. Indeed, some abolitionists insist that reform efforts are not just ineffective but legitimize an inherently dehumanizing and unjust practice.[4] In effect, they charge prison reformers, including those who might be well meaning, serious, and earnest, with complicity in maintaining an oppressive social practice.[5] Some abolitionists also argue that prison reform is a liberal-capitalist project that lacks the radical imagination needed to bring about a truly humane, democratic, and free society. These charges warrant thoughtful philosophical attention.

Philosophy, Punishment, and Prisons

At the heart of the vocation of philosophy is an inclination to consider radical ideas, to entertain the heretical thought, to not dismiss the "crazy" proposal. We should be open, even disposed, to questioning common sense and current arrangements, even when doing so is highly unpopular and poses some personal risk. Once we have thoroughly considered the radical thesis, we may find that we cannot accept it, that there are not compelling enough reasons to endorse it. We may nonetheless come away with a deeper appreciation of the relevant problems and possible solutions, and with a stronger grasp of what matters most.

For centuries, philosophers—Plato, Aquinas, Kant, Bentham, and many more—have written extensively about punishment and its justification. They have proposed and criticized theories based on retribution, deterrence, consent, forfeiture, fairness, reconciliation, rehabilitation, moral education, and other things. These philosophical theories typically abstract away from the concrete and grim realities of imprisonment, including the related questions of political economy and public finance. It is generally taken for granted that if penalties for criminal wrongdoing are legitimate, then a prison sentence is among the penalties that can be legitimately imposed. These theories also usually assume that the society within which imprisonment occurs is a just one (or nearly) and that the governing authority is fully legitimate. But what is yet to be shown—if it can be—is that imprisonment is a defensible practice in our own unjust society and world, or that it would be justified under better social conditions that we can realistically bring about.

Philosophers, legal scholars, and others have addressed the death penalty, and many are adamantly opposed to it, even when the offense is especially heinous.[6] The question of whether prisons should be abolished can be thought of in similar terms. Even if punishment as a practice is permissible, not all penalties are legitimate crime-control measures, notwithstanding that some crimes are serious. For example, few would accept torture and maiming as legitimate forms of punishment, even if they did help to prevent crime. We should also ask whether incarceration can be a legitimate penalty for a criminal offense.

We might formulate the issue by distinguishing two questions. First, can the practice of imprisonment be justified despite existing structural injustices (for example, institutional racism and economic injustice), or should the use of prisons be discontinued, wholly or in part, until these structural injustices have been corrected? Second, could the practice of imprisonment ever be justified in a just social order, or would a fully just society obviate the need for prisons and therefore make their use illegitimate and repugnant? These are the questions I will address.

This book takes up abolitionist ideas as philosophy. The reflections offered, sometimes critical, are my way of thinking through whether to adopt abolition as my own philosophical and political stance. I explore these thoughts with the hope they might help others decide whether to be reformers or abolitionists. My reflections have not led me to become an abolitionist, at least not in the most radical sense of that designation. But

I have learned much from thinking about abolitionist ideas, and I have changed my mind, at times fundamentally, about the practice of imprisonment under current conditions and in our possible futures. This critical encounter with the idea of prison abolition is therefore as much about explaining what I think abolitionists get right as it is about showing where I believe they go wrong. It is not my aim, then, to offer "the case against abolition" but rather to see what can be gained, philosophically and practically, from taking abolitionist ideas seriously.

Angela Davis and Black Critical Theory

Although all abolitionists share hostility toward prisons, abolitionist theory and practice is remarkably varied. Though broadly leftist in orientation, the radical anti-prison movement is not unified by an agreed-upon set of basic principles. There are black radical, Marxist, pacifist, feminist, post-structuralist, and anarchist strands of abolitionist thought, activism, and organizing. I do not survey or engage the full evolving constellation of ideas and arguments that self-described prison abolitionists have put forward.[7] I focus on the wide-ranging and hugely influential philosophical contributions of Angela Y. Davis.

Davis is the preeminent scholar-activist in the abolitionist movement, a prolific writer and defender of radical ideas, and a distinguished philosopher.[8] She is a key leader in the movement, and her work is a touchstone among abolitionists. In numerous books, essays, speeches, films, and interviews, Davis has defended a world without prisons as a morally required and realistic goal. Her anti-prison theorizing takes its shape within a distinctive and well-developed philosophical framework. And in the context of such theorizing, she asks vital philosophical questions, such as: "How do we imagine a better world and raise the questions that permit us to see beyond the given?"[9] Thinking about, and resisting, the practice of imprisonment has occupied Davis for more than fifty years. As she says, "a protracted engagement with the prison system has literally defined my life."[10]

Not all of Davis's writings on prisons focus on abolition. She critically engages prisons from a range of perspectives and for a variety of purposes. For instance, in her early intellectual and political development, she focused mainly on freeing political prisoners and exposing the ways that incarceration can be used as a mode of political repression (see Chapter 1). But in time she came to argue that prisons are obsolete.[11] This stance suggests that although prisons may have had some legitimate uses in the past, they are currently unnecessary, either because these legitimate functions can now be served in better and less costly ways or because there is no longer a need to have these functions served. Davis has also defended prison abolition as a necessary component of effective resistance to neoliberalism and as a key demand in a democratic socialist movement.[12] I take a broad view of what from her enormous corpus is relevant but concentrate on those writings that might plausibly be thought to support the thesis that prisons, even the "best" ones, should not exist—whether now, in the near future, or in a distant yet feasible utopia.

For Davis, talk of "abolition" rather than "reform" is not merely provocative rhetoric or the strategic hyperbole characteristic of some radical consciousness-raising discourse. Davis argues that a reform framework gives prisons unwarranted legitimacy and that what is needed is to convince people that states are not justified in using prisons and that justice demands that we work together to eliminate them. This position is made clear in a recent coauthored book on abolition feminism, where Davis and her collaborators write:

> What differentiates this explicitly abolitionist approach from prevailing ideas and scenarios addressing prison repression—both then and now—is the tenacious critique of prison reform and of criminal justice reform more broadly, as well as the recognition that the ideological impulse to contain all efforts to address the social damage wrought by prisons within the parameters of "reform" serves to further authorize incarceration as the legitimate and immutable foundation of justice.[13]

Moreover, Davis's language of "abolition" should not be interpreted as the propaganda of an elite vanguard of revolutionaries, nor as an expression of oracular wisdom from a charismatic leader who expects deference. Her organizing efforts are democratic, not demagogic. She seeks to work with others as equals, not to use them as unwitting instruments to the fulfillment of esoteric ideals. And in her writings, interviews, and public speaking, she proclaims her radical objectives openly and without apology.

Yet Davis does sometimes say things like the following:

> When we are told that we simply need better police and better prisons, we counter with what we really need. We need to reimagine security, which will involve the abolition of policing and imprisonment *as we know them*. We will say demilitarize the police, disarm the police, abolish the institution of the

police *as we know it*, and abolish imprisonment as the *dominant* mode of punishment [emphasis added].[14]

This kind of phrasing ("as we know it" and "as the dominant mode") could be interpreted as qualifying the call for prison and police abolition in ways that might make the distinction between abolition and reform seem unimportant or to be merely a verbal dispute. After all, many reformers also want to see policing and imprisonment radically changed. These qualifying phrases suggest that we might still rely on police, provided they were not armed with military-grade weapons, or that we might use prisons, provided they were not the *primary* form of crime control. Perhaps that is all some advocates mean by "abolition," a radical and evocative phrase that conjures up images of the abolitionist movement against chattel slavery but that, when stripped of rhetorical flourish, means no more than a call for fundamental change in law-enforcement practice. Yet that is not what Davis has in mind. Accordingly, I will explore prison abolition, not only in its more moderate versions, but primarily in its boldest and most radical form: a rejection of prison reform, even fundamental reform, as the ultimate goal; and a practical vision of a society and world that does not need or use prisons at all.[15]

Davis's critique of prisons is situated within a broader critique of racism, sexism, imperialism, and capitalism. She draws extensively on the traditions of Marxism, critical theory, feminism, and black radicalism. I too have been deeply influenced by these traditions of thought, and my discussion of abolition will largely operate within their parameters.

Much contemporary black radical thought, including black feminist theory, has been shaped by currents in Marxism, particularly by strains in critical theory. As a radical approach to studying and critiquing modern Western civilization, critical theory was forged in the 1920s and early 1930s at the Frankfurt-based Institute for Social Research (Institute für Sozialforschung), which was founded in 1923 and has long been regarded as the principal institutional site of the "Frankfurt School" tradition of critical theory. Herbert Marcuse, an early and prominent Frankfurt School theoretician, taught Angela Davis as an undergraduate (at Brandeis University), served as her dissertation advisor (at UC San Diego), and influenced her thought substantially. With Marcuse's encouragement, Davis studied Kant, Hegel, and Marx at the Institute in Frankfurt (then housed at Goethe University) from 1965 to 1967, where she attended lectures and participated in seminars conducted by Theodor W. Adorno, Jürgen Habermas, and other leading critical theorists. In subsequent years, and through a variety of books and essays, Davis developed her own approach to critical theory, which draws not only on Frankfurt School ideas but also on the broader Afro-modern intellectual tradition and radical feminist theory.

Black critical theorists, including Davis, rely primarily on historical analysis, social theory, cultural criticism, autobiographical narratives, personal experience, and experimental art to critique existing social arrangements and to communicate their transformative vision. True to their Frankfurt School roots, they generally avoid and are often suspicious of mainstream "positivist" empirical social science of the sort one generally encounters in U.S. departments of political science, sociology, and economics. Black critical theory is decidedly and consciously interdisciplinary, methodologically unconventional, and transgressive with respect to established academic norms.

Black critical theorists, like all critical theorists, are fundamentally concerned with liberating human beings from oppression. Though they value intellectual activity, *freedom* is their ultimate goal, and they believe radical structural transformation is needed to secure full liberation. Rejecting any sharp distinction between scholarship and political advocacy, their studies are not designed to be value-free, disinterested inquiry but forthrightly crafted to expose injustices, to defend the interests of the oppressed, and to highlight feasible paths to a better world. But they also, like earlier Marxists, tend not to engage in systematic moral theory or normative political philosophy of the sort typical in mainstream "analytic" philosophy departments.

Unlike the canonical figures of the Frankfurt School, black critical theorists are deeply influenced by black thinkers whom they deem part of what Cedric Robinson famously called "the black radical tradition."[16] Influential thinkers in this tradition include W.E.B. Du Bois, C.L.R. James, Claudia Jones, Frantz Fanon, Walter Rodney, and Angela Davis herself. This is a strand of the wider black political tradition that draws insights not only from Marxism, but also from revolutionary Black Nationalism, Afro-Caribbean radicalism, and Pan-African socialism. Black radicals are sharply critical of class stratification and capitalist labor exploitation but equally concerned with systemic racism and colonial subjugation. They do not pin their hopes for liberation on the leadership of the white working class but rather insist that those subjugated by white supremacy and Euro-American imperialism, including those relegated to slums, ghettos, and Bantustans around the world, are vital to any realistic hope for a truly free and democratic future.

Afro-Analytical Marxism and the Black Radical Tradition

The critical inquiry this book takes up is, in some ways, incongruous with the philosophical and political orientation of Davis and other black critical theorists. Some of what I have written—and the way I have written it—may strike many as perplexingly (and perhaps perversely) at cross purposes with those I am engaging. To reduce this dissonance (and at the risk of appearing pedantic), let me be explicit about how my approach to thinking about prison abolition differs from recent trends in black critical theory and abolitionist writings.

I consider myself part of the black radical tradition, not the least because my thinking has been profoundly shaped by the writings of Du Bois, the canonical black radical thinker.[17] But unlike some black critical theorists, I do not regard the black radical tradition as diametrically opposed to all forms of liberalism. I believe that core ideas drawn from liberal-egalitarian thought in particular merit steadfast defense—a bedrock commitment to an equal and extensive set of basic liberties for all, prioritizing the well-being of the worst off, tolerance for different conceptions of human flourishing, and limiting economic inequality to protect both democratic practices and meaningful opportunities to secure valued positions in social life. Liberalism and capitalism, in my view, need not stand or fall together, and "liberal socialism" is not a contradiction in terms. Here

I follow John Rawls in thinking that sound principles of justice are incompatible with welfare-state capitalism and are consistent only with either a property-owning democracy (essentially, egalitarian social democracy) or liberal market socialism. I also agree with Rawls that while basic individual liberties are of the utmost importance and have moral priority over fostering socioeconomic equality, the right to own means of production and to make market transactions for private gain are not basic liberties. These economic freedoms are justified only if they are to everyone's advantage and best promote the interests of the least well off in society.[18]

While I believe a philosophical approach that combines elements of liberal egalitarianism, Marxism, and black radicalism is exactly the approach that Du Bois took in works like *Black Reconstruction in America* (1935) and *Dusk of Dawn* (1940), my discussion of prison abolition will not rely primarily on liberal ideas or frameworks. Davis is a sharp critic of liberalism, and I prefer to take up her arguments largely on terms we both can accept.

Although I too have been influenced by Marxism and critical theory, in terms of method I am closer to G. A. Cohen's analytical Marxism and Habermas's critical theory than are many black radicals, including Davis. I believe it can be valuable, even indispensable, to make use of the tools of analytical philosophy and mainstream social science when critiquing existing social conditions and defending a vision of a just world.

I also believe that it is not enough to possess strong ethical convictions and moral courage, as vital as these are. Black critical theorists must also develop systematic moral arguments, not only against the status quo, but also for the radical social vision they favor. These arguments need not amount to a fully developed theory of justice. But they should have the capacity to persuade people who are open-minded but perhaps not yet convinced to accept black critical theorists' basic moral principles and not yet disposed to choose a radical solution to mutually acknowledged social problems.

Unlike many black critical theorists and Davis herself, I philosophize at some remove from political activism and social movements. I try to learn and accept criticism from any credible source of potential knowledge and wisdom, including from activists and movement leaders. This book is not, however, a commentary on the activities of the abolitionist movement. It is a book about ideas. Nor do I write in the role of a scholar-activist in an existing political struggle. Indeed, it would not be entirely unfair to describe me as part of the academic industrial complex that many black radicals ostensibly oppose.[19]

However, those who insist on a tighter connection between theory and practice (or between vision and praxis, to use the movement's idiom) may still find value in thinking these challenging questions through with me. I hope to present arguments they have yet to entertain or fully consider, arguments that may make a difference to their confidence in abolition or their skepticism toward it. No book is for everyone. *The Idea of Prison Abolition* is primarily for those still considering whether to insist that the practice of imprisonment can and should be improved or commit to fighting for abolition. It is a book premised on the notion that philosophical reflection can help us decide whether to join, champion, abandon, or oppose a cause. Philosophy has proven its value when it comes to thinking through the various dimensions of causes like animal rights, environmental justice, socialism, reproductive rights, reparations for slavery, multiculturalism, and ending global poverty. The cause of prison abolition is just as suitable a subject for philosophical engagement.

There is an additional value to this kind of critical interchange across philosophical and political traditions apart from how it bears on prison abolition. I favor pluralism when it comes to philosophical method. I think different approaches—phenomenology, critical theory, conceptual analysis, pragmatism, genealogy, reflective equilibrium, and so on—often yield complementary insights. And this book is an attempt at philosophical engagement across the continental-analytic divide—"Afro-analytical Marxism," as I call it.[20]

It is also valuable, though unfortunately too rare, to have open debate among those working in different political traditions of Afro-modern political thought. In recent years, one can't help but notice a general reluctance among black progressives and radicals to openly disagree with each other in print. To be sure, black conservatives and black "neoliberals" are relentlessly attacked, mocked, and dismissed. And those who try to "reduce" race to class are sometimes openly challenged. But debate within the broader black left is generally more muted, indirect, and infrequent; and when it does occur, it is often weighted down with ad hominem attacks or fueled by personal rivalry.

Yet we will make more progress in our thinking by directly testing our ideas with those who are not already inclined to accept them but who might be open to reconsidering their views. It is also good democratic practice, a way to maintain a healthy sense of our own fallibility and to prefigure the kind of social relations we hope to bring about. Indeed, black critical theory is already an amalgam of sometimes contending traditions, an approach forged through constructive debate and the exchange of ideas drawn from different philosophical frameworks. And I am convinced, and hope to persuade readers, that black critical theory, while vibrant and essential, needs to change in some ways if it is to realize its full transformative potential.

Lastly, there is, we must admit, a general reticence to openly disagree with our heroes. Angela Davis is an iconic, revered, and courageous figure on the left and in the black political tradition. Her work is thus seldom subjected to close critical scrutiny by those who are inspired by or admire her. But criticism, when honest and constructive, is not an insult. Hagiography is not the only way to honor our most cherished freedom fighters. On the contrary, it is out of respect for Davis's writings that I feel it necessary to engage with her ideas. Too often, Davis is treated as a mere symbol of black radicalism and militancy, like a raised fist or an Afro, as she herself laments.[21] As one of our most original and influential philosophers, she deserves the same kind of critical but respectful engagement that distinguished male or white philosophers regularly receive.

Reform or Abolition?

For reasons I will explain, prison abolition philosophy is utopian in ways that are both good and bad. Yet its utopianism is not my primary reason for not fully accepting prison abolition. Nor do my disagreements with this philosophy depend on rejecting socialism, much less defending capitalism. Rather, I continue to believe that incarceration has legitimate and socially necessary uses, including as punishment, and so prisons are not inherently unjust. Moreover, I think that the use of incarceration, under the right circumstances and in conjunction with other less harmful practices, can be worth its attendant risks and costs. I also believe that abolitionists' most compelling criticisms are properly directed, not at incarceration as such, but at background structural injustices in society, correctable failures of due process and prison administration, inhumane prison conditions, and inadequate public efforts to enable former prisoners to rejoin society on equal terms.

In saying that incarceration has legitimate uses, I am *not* defending U.S. federal, state, or municipal prison systems. These facilities are often grossly unjust and inhumane. They also contain many who have been confined for far too long, and many who should never have been imprisoned at all. Indeed, elsewhere I have questioned the legitimacy of the American criminal justice system.[22] Though I am not convinced that prisons are obsolete or approaching obsolescence, I strongly oppose U.S. mass incarceration, with its unprecedented and unrivaled rates of imprisonment and its highly punitive policies and unforgiving retributive ethos.[23] Still, there is a meaningful and important difference between, on the one hand, demanding such things as more humane prison conditions, less harsh prison sentences, and fewer prisoners and, on the other, insisting that there should be no prisons.

Some critics of prison reform write as if reformers seek merely to improve the criminal justice system but are not interested in or, in any case, are not committed to changing the basic structure of society.[24] Some abolitionists also charge reformers with viewing criminal law and law enforcement as the sole tools of crime control and harm prevention. I would not associate myself with either conception of reform. Not only must systemic injustice in the broader society be meaningfully addressed, but prison reform will not be successful without such redress. And crime can, and should, be controlled and prevented through a variety of means. Prisons are just one tool and best used, if at all, as a last resort.

Both reformers and abolitionists seek social change, sometimes the same changes (for example, greater protections for the lives, well-being, and health of prisoners). Indeed, some abolitionists are committed to what are sometimes called "non-reformist reforms"—that is, reforms that improve the lives and safety of prisoners but that will not strengthen, further legitimize, or expand prison systems.[25] The reformer, though, thinks the needed changes are consistent with preserving key features of the practice of imprisonment. The abolitionist, by contrast, believes the requisite changes require doing away with the practice of imprisonment completely or so transforming the practice that it would no longer be accurate to call it "imprisonment."

CHAPTER 1

Army of the Wronged: Political Prisoners and Black Radicalism

They daily stagger out of prison doors embittered, vengeful, hopeless, ruined. And of this army of the wronged, the proportion of Negroes is frightful. We protect and defend sensational cases where Negroes are involved. But the greater mass of arrested or accused Black folk have no defense. There is desperate need . . . to oppose this national racket of railroading to jails and chain gangs the poor, friendless and Black."

—W.E.B. DU BOIS, AS QUOTED IN *IF THEY COME IN THE MORNING: VOICES OF RESISTANCE* (1971)

In the late 1960s and early 1970s, a vigorous yet besieged black radical movement emerged in the United States. This was the volatile era of Black Power, and several black radicals (many affiliated with the Black Panther Party) explicitly regarded themselves as effectively at war with the U.S. government. These were left-wing revolutionaries convinced that the American social order completely lacked legitimacy and U.S. law therefore had no authority over them. They also thought that their declaration of war was reciprocated, that state officials—from the U.S. military to the FBI to local law enforcement—were consciously using the tactics and machinery of war to repress this internal uprising and socialist insurgency, including hunting, capturing, incapacitating, torturing, and killing black radicals. The prison is but one element, though a critical one, of the war machine.

Angela Davis's initial engagement with anti-prison theory and activism grows out of this historical context of revolutionary struggle against repressive and violent government action. Thus, her early radical opposition to the practice of imprisonment was mainly strategic or tactical. It was not primarily concerned with abolishing the prison as such. Her principal aim was to free oppressed communities, such as the inhabitants of urban ghettos, from economic exploitation and political subjugation. The idea of a political prisoner was central to this outlook, as some political prisoners were viewed as a vanguard in this struggle for emancipation. To understand the evolution of Davis's abolitionist stance, I look to the circumstances of her initial political formation, to her early efforts to free political prisoners (including herself), and to the ways that prisons are sometimes used for political repression and counterinsurgency.

There is much I agree with in Davis's early anti-prison standpoint, here understood as a political strategy and an analysis of the abuses of state power. I am also persuaded that the figure of the political prisoner can be a constructive lens for viewing black oppression more generally, particularly the injustices faced by ghetto denizens. To explore these ideas in more depth, highlighting what is most relevant for thinking about today's anti-prison theory and practice, let's examine some classic autobiographical writings in the tradition of black radicalism from this period. George Jackson, Huey P. Newton, Assata Shakur, and Davis herself each spent significant time in jail or prison. While incarcerated they wrote about their lives, their captivity, and their radical political vision. They regarded themselves as political prisoners and, effectively, as prisoners of war, captured by the enemy and hoping to escape to rejoin the fight. Though each fought for their own personal freedom from incarceration and for the freedom of other political prisoners, their stated aim was ultimately the freedom of all oppressed peoples through revolutionary struggle.

Slavery, Colonialism, and the Right to Revolt

The enslavement of Africans and their descendants in the Americas are a literary, moral, and political touchstone for these four black radicals. Each regards militant slave resistance and the radical abolitionist movement as models for their own political engagement and as inspiration in their struggle for freedom. It is tempting, then, to regard their autobiographical, prison-related writings as neo-slave narratives.[1] After all, they rely on familiar slave-narrative conventions. For instance, they provide detailed and vivid descriptions of the horrifically inhumane conditions of their captivity and the cruelty of their captors. Their first-person narration includes harrowing attempts to evade capture, with suspenseful escapes facilitated by guile and uncommon bravery. An emotional identification with the protagonist is created through lyrical and evocative representations of the fear, sadness, and paranoia of the fugitive. There are scenes depicting painful shackling, public humiliation, brutal beatings, heartbreaking separation from loved ones, and torturous physical isolation. The sympathetic reader of these writings is moved by displays of solidarity and self-respect among the oppressed; inspired by the sacrifice and commitment of allies; and disappointed by the inevitable betrayal and cowardly submission of those well positioned to advance the cause.

Yet, I am hesitant to interpret these works solely through the lens of that venerable tradition of black letters. The most influential slave narratives, such as those of Frederick Douglass and Harriet Jacobs, exposed and dramatized the evils of slavery with a view toward moral suasion. They were self-conscious appeals to the sympathy, conscience, or Christian morals of powerful whites, with the hope that they might withdraw their support for the slave regime and join the nonviolent abolitionist movement. The autobiographical writings of the black radical political prisoners I discuss are not best understood as attempts at moral suasion or peaceful protest. And they are aimed at raising the political consciousness of the oppressed, not at appealing to the powerful for redress. They are their own genre of literary nonfiction, which could be called "revolutionary political-prisoner narratives" or "radical prisoner narratives," and I will treat them as such, highlighting what is most distinctive and compelling about this mode of writing.

Nevertheless, slavery and slave revolts are frequently invoked in these writings. The abolitionist heroes here are not Douglass or Jacobs but Nat Turner and Harriet Tubman, and sometimes

John Brown. The references to enslavement and slave resistance play four principal roles. First, the ongoing mistreatment of black people, in black communities and in prison, is said to be the continuation of slavery, a new form of slavery, or strikingly like familiar practices of enslavement. Second, the defiance of the political prisoner or fugitive from the law is regarded as having the same moral and political grounds as the defiance of the fugitive slave. Third, the condition of enslavement—in particular, the relation between the slaveholder and the enslaved—is taken to justify extralegal, even violent, resistance, as self-defense and to secure emancipation. And finally, slave rebellions are treated as a model for revolutionary collective action, both inside and outside prison walls.

In addition to slavery, colonial subjugation is frequently invoked in these radical prison narratives, and for the same reasons. Black American oppression is often portrayed as akin to colonial domination, with blacks in the United States described as a subject people with a right to self-determination that has long been, and continues to be, wrongfully denied. Life in American ghettos, a highly visible symbol of black degradation, is often described as the "internal colonization" of the dispossessed. The violent and despotic relation between the colonizer and the colonized (like the relation between master and slave) is taken as a justification for defiance of law and for organized rebellion. And revolutionary national liberation movements in Africa, Asia, and Latin America are models for political engagement to win black American independence, through violent struggle if necessary. Here, two earlier texts in the broader black radical tradition are hugely influential—Frantz Fanon's *The Wretched of the Earth* (1961) and *The Autobiography of Malcolm*

X (1965)—and are best read alongside these black radical prison narratives to grasp their full import, and to see how black nationalist and revolutionary socialist ideas are combined. Let me break down the two narrative patterns (slavery analogies and colonial parallels) to make explicit the underlying structure of moral argument they contain.

Slavery, in both the republican and liberal traditions, is regarded as intolerable tyranny, abject unfreedom, and a state of war against the enslaved. There are two related wrongs—despotism and involuntary servitude—which are often combined in practice. This miserable condition, says the black radical, has been the fate of generations of black people in America and elsewhere: involuntary servitude under despotic rule. To add insult to injury, this tyrannical and exploitative practice was justified on the grounds that black people are an inferior race and are incapable of rational autonomy, and therefore are owed no better treatment than permanent paternalistic subjugation. For nearly four centuries, the principal agents and beneficiaries of this wretched regime have been intent on maintaining white supremacy at the expense of peoples of African descent. Thus, the long-standing plight of black people in the United States and in the Americas more broadly has been involuntary servitude under despotic white rule.

In *Soledad Brother: The Prison Letters of George Jackson* (1970), George Jackson writes to his father, "I know you have never been free. I know that few blacks over here have ever been free. The forms of slavery merely *changed* at the signing of the Emancipation Proclamation from chattel slavery to economic slavery."[2] In a letter to his mother, Jackson continues on this theme by insisting that black people continue to be "slaves" and inheritors of a "neoslave existence."[3] At the same time, he speaks of black Americans as being in a "colonial situation," as members of a "black colony," and as forcibly socialized and educated within an "enemy culture."[4]

Jackson explicitly rejected Martin Luther King Jr.'s nonviolent resistance on the grounds that black people's oppressors have no fellow feeling or sense of justice toward their subordinates, are manifestly hypocritical in their stated commitment to "liberty" and "equality," and will not yield without the use of force.[5] To further establish the legitimacy of this point of view, he draws attention to the fact that eighteenth-century white colonial settlers in North America refused to submit to the arbitrary will of the English monarchy, publicly declared their independence, and, when threatened with violent reprisals, fought a war to secure their freedom and political autonomy.[6] Black Americans, though subject to much worse forms of tyranny and servitude, are consistently denied self-determination, and are broadly condemned or even retaliated against when they fight back or refuse to submit.

In *Revolutionary Suicide* (1973), Huey Newton highlights the similarities between enslavement and imprisonment.[7] He describes prison labor as uncompensated involuntary servitude. He notes the lack of freedom of movement, the absolute power of prison authorities, the constant surveillance, and the general atmosphere of fear and suspicion. He tells us, "if inmates develop meaningful and revolutionary friendships among themselves, these ties are broken by institutional transfer, just as the slavemaster broke up families."[8] He also laments the fact that black children are not taught that their ancestors participated in slave rebellions.[9]

We see a similar pattern in Assata Shakur's radical prison narrative. Shakur was convicted of murdering a New Jersey state trooper but later escaped from prison and fled to Cuba, where she reportedly remains, having been granted political asylum. In *Assata: An Autobiography* (1988), she explains that she came to reject her "slave name" of "JoAnne Deborah Chesimard" in favor of "Assata," which means "she who struggles."[10] She too invokes slavery and slave revolts, including a nod to her hero Harriet Tubman, who also renamed herself. But more often Shakur uses an anti-colonial framework to characterize her revolutionary activity: "[The Black Panther] Party supported revolutionary struggles and governments all over the world and insisted the u.s. get out of Africa, out of Asia, out of Latin America, and out of the ghetto too."[11] In line with this framing, she considers herself a member of the "Black Liberation Army," whose purpose is to deliver national liberation for a colonially subordinated people "by any means necessary."[12] The moral ground for this stance is not only opposition to racism and capitalism but also a belief that black self-determination is a "basic right."[13]

These imprisoned radicals insist on the right to revolution in response to unyielding tyranny and exploitation. Sometimes the apt comparison is to the American Revolutionary War, particularly when the colonial subjugation analogy is being invoked. At other times, the relevant comparison is to the U.S. Civil War, which was waged, in part, over slavery. In both cases, the rhetorical point of the comparison is to highlight the fact that the black liberation struggle, even when revolutionary in its aims, is not morally out of step with American political culture but is in fact a logical extension of it, though, crucially, in an antiracist and anti-imperialist register.

Law Enforcement as a Weapon of War

In her 2000 foreword to Shakur's *Assata*, Angela Davis explains: "When Richard Nixon raised the slogan of 'law and order' in the 1970s, it was used in part to discredit the black liberation movement and to justify the deployment of the police, courts, and prisons against key figures in this and other radical movements of that era."[14] A close reading of these black radical narratives reveals a shared outlook on the nature and function of law enforcement in the United States. Law-enforcement agencies—what Davis calls the "police-court-prison apparatus"—are viewed as organized violence that functions to repress or thwart political rebellion.[15] We are not talking about mere ordinary failures of due process, say, because of incompetence or bias. These are coordinated efforts to maintain a system of domination and exploitation in response to militant dissent and active opposition.

The police are the first line of defense and the public face of state violence against rebellious oppressed populations. In an influential anthology of prison writings, *If They Come in the Morning: Voices of Resistance* (1971), edited by Angela Davis, Davis says: "From Birmingham to Harlem to Watts, Black ghettos are occupied, patrolled, and often attacked by massive deployments of police. The police, domestic caretakers of violence, are the oppressor's emissaries, charged with the task of containing us within the boundaries of our oppression."[16] When the police are visible in black communities, they are generally perceived to be present, not to protect and serve the community, but rather, as Shakur remarks, to function as "nothing but a foreign, occupying army, beating, torturing, and murdering people at whim and without restraint."[17] The Black Panthers initially garnered the respect and trust of those in black communities because they monitored the police during traffic stops to deter law-enforcement officers from engaging in illegal searches, harassment, and unwarranted violence. They would not only carry legal firearms but criminal law books, which they would read from aloud to make onlookers and the police themselves aware of how constitutional rights to due process were being violated.

Newton brings the point home vividly by narrating the police encounter that led to him being shot and then imprisoned for almost three years.[18] In the early morning hours, he and a friend, Gene McKinney, were driving around in search of some "righteous soul food" after a night of partying and socializing with family and friends. Newton noticed the red light of a police car behind them and pulled over. When the officer got to their car window, he immediately made it clear that he knew who Newton was. Shortly thereafter, another police car arrived. Newton was ordered to get out of the car, and when he did, he took his law book with him, as was his practice. He was physically searched in a way that Newton felt was degrading, and afterwards he protested that the officer had no grounds to arrest him and proceeded to read from the relevant part of his law book. The officer responded, "You can take that book and shove it up your ass, nigger," and then struck Newton with a "solid straight-arm," knocking him to the ground. As Newton rose, the officer pulled out his gun and shot Newton in the stomach. Newton heard a few more shots and then blacked out. He later learned that an officer, John Frey, was killed during the encounter and that he was charged with Frey's murder. (Newton was found guilty of voluntary manslaughter in 1967, but the conviction was overturned on appeal in 1970.)

Although police are the most feared and despised, black radicals do not trust the courts either. Prosecutors seek convictions on fabricated or flimsy evidence and use the threat of long sentences to extract unfair plea bargains. Judges deny bail or set it at unreachable heights. They also run trials in ways that favor the state's case; and they impose excessive penalties upon conviction. Juries, when properly composed of peers, can sometimes be sympathetic. But more often they are overwhelmingly (if not exclusively) white, strongly biased against black defendants, or manipulated by clever and unscrupulous prosecutors. It was the reasonable fear that a black radical could not get a fair trial in the United States that led Angela Davis to flee when charged with murder, kidnapping, and conspiracy.

Relying exclusively on Davis's account, as presented in *Angela Davis: An Autobiography* (1974), the basic background to her famous case is this. George Jackson was one of three "Soledad Brothers" being held in Soledad Correctional Facility in California on the charge that they killed a prison guard. Davis was a member of the Soledad Brothers Defense Committee, a group of activists fighting to free the Soledad Brothers on grounds that they were political prisoners and innocent of the charges against them. Jonathan Jackson and George Jackson were brothers and, due to her work to free political prisoners, Davis became close friends and comrades with them. In what Davis calls a "courthouse revolt," Jonathan (at seventeen) entered the Marin County Courthouse during an ongoing trial, armed with a carbine. He, together with three other San Quentin prisoners present in the courtroom, took several court officials and jurors hostage. Jonathan was shot to death by prison guards as they attempted to leave the scene. A judge was also killed and a prosecutor wounded in this encounter. Although Davis was not present, her .380 automatic handgun was used during the courthouse revolt. Court officials contended that Jonathan had taken this drastic action as part of a plan to bargain for the freedom of his brother George and that Davis, because of her passionate love for George, had conspired in the effort.

When Davis learned that the state sought her arrest, she immediately went into hiding, but decided not to leave the country. Relying on disguises, assisted by trusted friends and comrades, and moving around under the cover of night, she fled from Los Angeles, to Las Vegas, to Chicago, to Detroit, to New York City, and to Miami to evade capture. During this time as a fugitive, the FBI put her on its "Most Wanted" list. She was ultimately discovered and arrested in a motel in New York. She was then temporarily incarcerated at the Women's House of Detention in New York, where Davis and Bettina Aptheker began working together to produce the anthology that would become *If They Come in the Morning*, which was explicitly conceived as "an organizing weapon."[19] Davis was later extradited, with the help of the U.S. military, to California to stand trial.

Though Davis would eventually be granted bail, she did not flee again. This is somewhat surprising. Just prior to her release on bond, George Jackson had been killed by San Quentin prison guards under suspicious circumstances. Davis believed that Jackson had been murdered because of his political beliefs and because of his radicalizing influence on other prisoners. "George was," as she says, "a symbol of the will of all of us behind bars, and of that strength which oppressed people always seem to be able to pull together."[20] With his death at the hands of state officials, Davis had to worry that she could be next. Moreover, she had no real faith in the fairness of the judicial system, and no black jurors participated in deciding her guilt or innocence (the one black person in the jury pool was preemptively challenged by the prosecution). It is true that, during her confinement, the California Supreme Court abolished the death penalty, and so she was no longer charged with a capital crime (which, as it happens, is the reason she became eligible for bail). But like Jackson, she too could be killed in prison or isolated for years in solitary confinement. (California voters reinstated the death penalty in 1978.)

The reasons that Davis thought she could win in court and the reasons for why she took the risk of fighting her case are revealing. The courtroom is itself a battleground on which radicals and the state wage war against one another. Yes, sometimes brute force is used, as in the tragic case of Jonathan Jackson or the police shooting of Huey Newton. But often the law itself can be deployed tactically—for repression, or for liberation. In the preface to *If They Come in the Morning*, Davis and Aptheker say: "The courtroom victories thus far are the result of uncompromising and relentless resistance: one which succeeded in altering the political consciousness of the jurors in particular, and the communities in general; one which politically, organizationally and legally at every point and opportunity, sought to counter the calculated assault of the government."[21]

The key to success in court was to help jurors see the merit of the larger political cause and to expose publicly how the state was using any means at its disposal, legal or illegal, to repress the movement by incapacitating its most vital and effective leaders. Davis explicitly sought lawyers who would see her case as "political" and would understand that "the courtroom battle would be interwoven with a battle conducted by a mass movement."[22] She and her lawyers intentionally avoided moving Davis's case to federal court and instead successfully petitioned to have her case moved to California state court. The main reason was that, in federal court, the judge questions and picks the jurors, but in state court the defense would participate in voir dire, allowing them to weed out racist and anti-communist jurors and to impanel mostly working-class people.[23] Davis also successfully petitioned to be co-counsel in her case, and she delivered the opening statement, in which she explained to the jury "how [her] activities around the defense of the Soledad Brothers were part of a history of involvement in the movement to defend and free political prisoners such as Huey Newton, the New York Panther 21, Bobby Seale and Ericka Huggins, the Los Angeles Panther 18 and the seven other brothers from Soledad Prison also charged with killing a guard."[24] Davis was ultimately acquitted on all counts of the indictment.

High-profile court cases that sought to free political prisoners were also good for the movement itself. There were huge rallies, around the globe, calling for the release of Huey Newton and Angela Davis. These assemblies were opportunities to bring more people into the movement, to engage in political education, to enhance public awareness of the malfeasance and malice of the "police-court-prison apparatus," and to raise money for bail and lawyers for political prisoners. When a case was won, the victory galvanized the movement by providing evidence that the resistance of ordinary people could make a difference. For those incarcerated black radicals, this open public agitation could also lift their spirits, giving them much needed hope. Remarking on the day of her initial capture, and facing the death penalty, Davis says, "Yet, at that moment, I was feeling better than I had felt in a long time. The struggle would be difficult, but there was already a hint of victory. In the heavy silence of the jail, I discovered that if I concentrated hard enough, I could hear echoes of slogans being chanted on the other side of the walls. 'Free Angela Davis.' 'Free All Political Prisoners.'"[25]

Political Prisoners and Prisoners of War

So what, then, makes a person a "political prisoner"? George Jackson, universally regarded as a political prisoner among black radicals, analyzed two different types of mindset. There is the ordinary "criminal mentality," which Jackson exhibited as a child when, without political intent, he engaged in many unlawful acts, including robbery and hijacking, because he simply couldn't accommodate himself to social rules that he regarded as oppressive: "All my life I've done exactly what I wanted to do just when I wanted, no more, perhaps less sometimes, but never any more, which explains why I had to be jailed."[26] In prison at eighteen years old, and with a life sentence, he read the classics of Marxist theory and guerrilla warfare, which he says "redeemed" him, and he became friends with and learned from other prison radicals. Behind bars, Jackson underwent a political transformation, from someone with a "criminal mentality" to someone with a "revolutionary mentality." He took it as his mission to educate fellow prisoners and to organize them into an "implacable army of liberation."[27] In response, prison authorities worked to isolate him and to limit his influence on other prisoners.

In an essay composed while she was being held at Marin County Jail (included in *If They Come in the Morning*), Davis argues that a political prisoner is an incarcerated person who has broken a law that directly or indirectly oppresses a group, and breaks that law, not for selfish reasons, but in order to ensure the well-being or liberation of the oppressed group.[28] The ordinary criminal, though perhaps oppressed, breaks the law solely for personal gain. The political prisoner takes unlawful actions, at least in part, to relieve the unjust burdens of the oppressed or to change society for the better. The political prisoner's unlawful actions must, in one way or another, convey a protest against the existing social order, and this open resistance must be part of the reason they are, or remain, imprisoned.

A second kind of political prisoner, on Davis's view, makes use of lawful means to organize and move people to resist oppression. The political actor in this case has broken an "unwritten law" that prohibits challenging the status quo. False charges are then brought against them to justify their incarceration. Fundamentally, then, it is the effort to organize and mobilize the masses for their liberation—whether legally or illegally, and whether inside or outside prison—that gives rise to state repression. As the movement grows, "the judicial system and its extension, the penal system, consequently become key weapons in the state's fight to preserve the existing conditions of class domination, therefore racism, poverty and war."[29] "Crime" is merely the pretext for their captivity, a way to discredit the political prisoner. Thus, on this account, Martin Luther King Jr. and George Jackson, despite their disagreements over the morality and effectiveness of political violence, were both political prisoners.

In Newton's "Prison, Where Is Thy Victory?" (his contribution to *If They Come in the Morning*), he distinguishes between two types of prisoners.[30] The first type, which he calls "illegitimate capitalist," does not deny the legitimacy of the society's laws but seeks to acquire money and power through illegal means. The second type contends that the society is deeply unjust and its laws illegitimate. This kind of prisoner refuses to exploit and degrade others for private gain but feels no obligation to comply with the law. In fact, this type of prisoner refuses to cooperate with the oppressive system except insofar as such cooperation would help hasten the system's demise. This second type of prisoner, Newton maintains, is a political prisoner, whether they have acquired this radical outlook prior to or during their confinement.

In *Revolutionary Suicide*, Newton acknowledges that, like Jackson, he was once an ordinary criminal or, in his parlance, an "illegitimate capitalist."[31] Once he became a black radical and started the Black Panther Party (with Bobby Seale), he worked to politicize street hustlers who operated in the underground economy of illegal activity—in effect, to convert them from illegitimate capitalists to anti-capitalists—and some came to contribute weapons and money to the party and volunteered in the party's community service programs. Though Newton's earlier periods in jail were not the occasion for his political transformation, his previous stints in prison, along with his experience organizing "brothers on the block," did prepare him for his long confinement as a political prisoner, during which he sought to instill "the spirit of revolution" among the prison population.

Indeed, Newton did not draw a sharp separation, either theoretically or practically, between life in the ghetto and life in prison. Exploitation, confinement, segregation, violence, and surveillance typify both socio-spatial sites, and the war against the rebellious few takes place on both terrains. The ghetto uprising in Watts and the prison uprising at Attica (both sometimes called "riots") are kin. As are police in black communities and guards in prisons.

This position is echoed by Shakur, who laments to a fellow prisoner at Middlesex County Jail that "the only difference between here [prison] and the streets is that one is maximum security and the other is minimum security. The police patrol our communities just like the guards patrol here. I don't have the faintest idea how it feels to be free."[32] But out of these same oppressed communities come "black revolutionaries," who are created in part by harsh ghetto conditions, but also in prisons "like attica, san quentin, bedford hills, leavenworth, and sing sing."[33] Shakur insists that prisons are used as weapons in a "genocidal war against Black and Third World people."[34] This is why a Black Liberation Army is necessary, for both self-defense and emancipation.

Expanding the conception of "prison" to include the ghetto, as these radical prison narratives suggest, opens up a theoretical possibility that bears on how we should think about the relationship between law (including its enforcement and defiance) and war. If ghettos are, in the relevant respects, also prisons, then this might be reason to expand the concept of "political prisoner" to include ghetto denizens who regard the sociopolitical order as oppressive and consequently refuse to cooperate with its laws and norms. They have either engaged in unlawful resistance (for example, participating in the underground economy) or violated the "unwritten law" that prohibits even lawful resistance. This kind of political prisoner is a denizen of the ghetto who, because of unjust economic disadvantage or racial discrimination, lacks the freedom to move from a ghetto to a neighborhood where they could enjoy all the advantages of equal citizenship, including freedom from impoverishment, racism, and police harassment. Not only would the police-court-prison apparatus then be properly understood as a weapon of war, but those relegated to prison *as an institutional site of punitive incarceration* (for example, San Quentin) would be prisoners of war. They would be combatants who have been captured during an ongoing civil conflict.

One possible problem with this political analysis is that black denizens of the ghetto during the Black Power era were not confined to the ghetto because they openly struggled against the status quo. Yes, there were those, like Shakur, who out of solidarity refused to leave black communities: "I want to help free the ghetto, not run away from it, leaving my people behind."[35] Yet the vast majority were stuck in these deeply disadvantaged and segregated communities because they were *black*, not because they had a "revolutionary mentality"; and they could not exit these neighborhoods even if they accommodated themselves to the injustices of the system and didn't fight back. Thus, in one crucial respect, ghetto denizens are not like the political prisoners depicted in these black radical narratives.

However, some residents of ghettos, then and now, are defiant in the relevant respects, and this resistance is sometimes the cause of their ghetto confinement. Those who refuse to participate in the licit economy on the grounds that to do so would be degrading or exploitative often have great difficulty raising sufficient funds to move to better neighborhoods, particularly if they abstain from preying on other disadvantaged members of their community (for example, not robbing them or selling them harmful narcotics). Their unwillingness to accept whatever jobs are available is "punished" with an impoverished and segregated existence. Some of these rebellious residents will have criminal or arrest records, making it challenging for them to find jobs or decent housing. I am therefore inclined to endorse an additional subcategory of political prisoners to include them. This would bring new meaning to the slogan "Free All Political Prisoners," as it would require abolishing the ghetto as a socio-spatial site of oppression.[36]

Black Radicalism and the Struggle to "Abolish" Prisons

As I will discuss in the chapters to come, Davis develops her abolitionist philosophy over time to include the claims that prisons are inherently dehumanizing and exploitative and that they would be unnecessary in a just society and peaceful world.[37] But her early opposition to prisons is based on her contention, shared by many black radical thinkers, that prisons represent formidable obstacles to mass mobilization to transform society. She argues that prisons are instruments of war and political repression. Though prisons are sometimes used to punish "ordinary criminals," they are often used to maintain an unjust status quo and to put down any significant political resistance. This is a critical point that Davis and other black radicals hope to communicate through their prison-related writings, and this critical analysis should be seriously considered, and can be consistently embraced, even by those who are convinced that prisons can also serve legitimate functions. Prison reformers and abolitionists can learn from it.

Thus, I will close this chapter by considering how these radical prison narratives conceive of prisons as a tactical terrain on which political prisoners and their allies fight it out against a repressive political regime. Just as there are tactical advantages to be gained over the police and the courts, it is possible—through organizing, political education, and prisoner solidarity—to considerably weaken the power of prisons as a weapon against the oppressed. There is, in effect, a way for the "army of the wronged" to partially *disarm* their adversaries, as a means of self-defense. This kind of war maneuver could be understood as a component of a long-range plan to ultimately do away with prisons altogether. But it can also be an element of a prison reform agenda.

The principal strategy here is to make the use of prisons for political repression self-defeating. There's an inside game and an outside game. With respect to the internal life of prisons, the black radical movement sets out to demonstrate that repression through incarceration will not deter their militant political activity. Nor is it an effective means of incapacitating incarcerated political rebels. Part of the reason prisons fail to deter ghetto denizens from lawbreaking is that they are already living in a "minimum security prison," and so may feel they have little to lose by being defiant. As Jackson says, "Blackmen born in the U.S. and fortunate enough to live past the age of eighteen are conditioned to accept the inevitability of prison. For most of us, it simply looms as the next phase in a sequence of humiliations."[38] But the principal means of showing that prisons won't deter resistance is by continuing and even expanding political agitation, organization, and education inside prisons. Though captured and caged, the dissident will not submit or lay down arms, even if this means a longer prison stay and greater suffering while incarcerated. Political prisoners insist that they are not in need of "rehabilitation," as there is nothing wrong with them. It is a broken social system that needs to be fixed, or perhaps replaced.

As already discussed, political prisoners seek to turn ordinary criminals into political prisoners. After their consciousness has been raised, radicalized prisoners may be urged to disobey prison rules or prison guards' commands. They may, for instance, refuse to submit to strip searches, fashion makeshift weapons, or go on hunger strikes. Another tactic is to refrain from routine prison labor, such as preparing food, cleaning, and doing laundry. Prisoner strikes are all the more meaningful, from a political point of view, when they include refusing to provide goods and services for the benefit of private firms or others outside the prison. This conscious withdrawal of labor not only disrupts the order of prisons but also expresses a broader political message about labor exploitation in society. Shakur advances this position when she tells the story of a prison guard confronting her with "a big bushel of stringbeans":

> "Here, we want you to snap these stringbeans." "How much are you gonna pay me?" i asked. "We don't pay no inmate nothin', but if you snap these beans we'll let your door stay open while you snap them." "I don't work for nothing. I ain't gonna be no slave for nobody."[39]

Newton was similarly defiant while in prison, viewing his resistance as a way of instilling or strengthening a spirit of revolution among his fellow prisoners: "I look forward to the time when all inmates will offer greater resistance by refusing to work as I did. Such a simple move would bring the machinery of the penal system to a halt."[40] In effect, this kind of in-prison resistance turns the socio-spatial conditions of the prison into a radicalizing force, an incubator of militants; and because the vast majority of prisoners are at some point released, this revolutionary spirit spreads to the streets. The formerly incarcerated bring what they've learned in prison to family, friends, and associates, further developing the social movement.

When there is sufficient shared political consciousness, sense of purpose, and solidarity among prisoners in a particular facility, a prison uprising may be organized with a view, not just to improving prison conditions, but to advancing a political cause. For instance, the 1971 prisoner rebellion at Attica Correctional Facility in New York began two weeks after the killing of George Jackson at San Quentin.[41] In Davis's reflections on the meaning of the Attica "revolt," she argues that it awakened and enlivened the political passions of the people, for it exposed the murderous intent of state actors. She also says that "the revolt was particularly edifying in that it burst forth as if to demonstrate that the brutal killing of George Jackson fell dismally short of its repressive aim."[42]

With respect to the outside game, the aim of imprisoned black radicals is to encourage and strengthen solidarity between the dispossessed who aren't incarcerated and those who are locked up, particularly political prisoners. This is achieved, in part, by destigmatizing criminal offending, imprisonment, and felony convictions. Being susceptible or driven to crime and thereby vulnerable to being incarcerated is a component of black people's subjugation, not merely a result of bad character or poor upbringing as racist ideology would lead some to believe. But fostering such solidarity is also accomplished by making a compelling case that political prisoners do not deserve to be in prison and thus that "retribution" is not warranted. The state wants the public to believe that these would-be revolutionaries are common criminals to be feared and loathed. This attempt to delegitimize their political struggle must be countered or else the state will be free to destroy them with impunity.

Poor and working-class black people who have been involuntarily segregated in ghettos have had many negative, and sometimes violent, experiences with law enforcement, and they know that many who end up in prison were deeply disadvantaged before their convictions and often committed their crimes because of limited opportunities and out of economic desperation. They are not inclined to see the police-court-prison apparatus as friendly to the interests of the oppressed. As Davis argues, because of the experience of black people in ghettos, "an almost instinctive affinity binds the mass of Black people to the political prisoners."[43]

What ordinary black folk typically lack, though, is a theoretical framework that helps them understand their situation. They also lack a feasible strategy for defeating their oppressors or for lifting the weight of their oppression. This the political prisoner tries to provide through revolutionary theory and practice. But, in addition, political prisoners show, through their open agitation and willingness to risk being "punished," that they are actively working to transform the social order and are prepared to sacrifice all to achieve this end. They represent a threat to the system, which is why they must be silenced and made an example of.

Their obvious "skin in the game" makes it easier for oppressed people to trust and side with them. Because these political prisoners are viewed as providing vital leadership and are regarded as heroic figures, black people are invested in and willing to contribute to the struggle to free them.

Predictably, prison officials will attempt to neutralize the most influential political prisoners by relocating them to solitary confinement (the prison within the prison). The point of this action, black radicals argue, is to sharply curtail their influence on other prisoners. By making it challenging to communicate with other prisoners, prison officials impede political prisoners' ability to coordinate collective action and to provide political education. Sometimes the use of solitary confinement for political prisoners will backfire, causing other prisoners to protest and spurring unrest in the facility. If this response is intense and enduring, it may be sufficient to get the political prisoner released back into the general prison population. But even if not, it may spread or deepen the spirit of resistance among prisoners, perhaps giving birth to new leaders among them. Solitary confinement can also hurt a radical movement's cause outside prison walls. This is where publishing books like *Soledad Brother* and *If They Come in the Morning* becomes crucial. Political prisoners in isolation are then able to get their revolutionary vision to the people, who may rally to their defense.

Given their primary intended audience—oppressed people of color—the fact that radical prison narratives are first-person accounts of experiences with law enforcement is not incidental. These testimonials often resonate more powerfully than a theoretical treatise or political pamphlet would. To serve their purposes, they require, if not a charismatic person at their center, at least an authentic and credible voice. The self-sacrifice and resolve in fighting for the oppressed must be readily apparent. The autobiographical background often helps to establish this. It also enables the writer to be a likeable protagonist in a dramatic story with heroes and villains, tragedies and triumphs. As a result, it is harder to paint the political prisoner as a monster, someone to be killed or permanently incapacitated. Moreover, the moral lessons that such works seek to impart are often more effectively communicated to a broad audience through moral exemplars than through abstract principles. In all these respects and others, black radical narratives are similar in form to traditional slave narratives.

Yet, the differences are worth emphasizing. Although both genres are political autobiographies, slave narratives are exercises in moral persuasion, while black radical narratives aim at fomenting revolution. The primary audience is also different. Slave narratives were aimed at powerful whites, while black radical narratives are targeted at the oppressed. They both advance a political ethics—nonviolent resistance versus an ethic of revolt. The fugitive slave and the political prisoner both break the law to advance the cause of freedom. However, black radical narratives emphasize how the law can be a useful (if limited) weapon in a tactical struggle. Finally, war, in the form of civil conflict, but also of anti-imperial resistance, is the primary framework for black revolutionaries, who believe only an army of the wronged have a chance, however slim, at victory.

CHAPTER 2

The Uses and Abuses of Incarceration: Punishment, Dehumanization, and Slavery

Black radical anti-prison theory has deep roots, initially arising out of concerted efforts to free political prisoners, resist political repression, and defend against the increasingly warlike machinery of law enforcement. Today's critiques of prisons have grown more complex, encompassing a wider range of objections to the practice. Consider Angela Davis. Since her incarceration at Marin County Jail and her ultimate acquittal, the philosopher and scholar-activist's opposition to prisons has been less about open revolutionary conflict with the state, and more focused on a critique of the practice of imprisonment and the social conditions that (appear to) make this practice necessary. This book, in essence, grew out of my examination of these and other abolitionist criticisms.

Let's begin with two of Davis's most influential objections to the prison system. These objections make clear why the term "abolition"—given its nod to celebrated attempts to end the dehumanizing practice of slavery—is regarded as the appropriate language to demand an end to the use of prisons. Davis maintains that imprisonment is a dehumanizing practice, a form of treatment that no human being, regardless of their behavior or attitudes, should be subjected to. She also argues that prisons, in the United States at least, are linked to the practice of slavery in ways that make imprisonment deeply objectionable, and particularly intolerable for African Americans. There is merit and insight in each of these objections. So let's consider their strengths and weaknesses and whether they provide sufficient grounds to reject a prison-reform framework or to end the practice of imprisonment. But before turning to that examination, we need greater clarity about our principal subject—prison.

What Is a Prison?

In 1946, Malcolm X was imprisoned at the Charlestown State Prison in Massachusetts. Describing his experience there in his famous autobiography, he noted how his official prison number came to displace his name and truncated his identity, and that this was a common and degrading experience for prisoners adapting to institutional life. He also said that the bars of his cell made an indelible mark on his mind, making him feel like he was in a cage, and that cell bars were an impediment to any kind of rehabilitation. Prisoners readily purchased illegal drugs and other contraband from unscrupulous guards, and they were forced to make license plates for the state as part of their work assignments. Malcolm remarked: "The cells didn't have running water. The prison had been built in 1805—in Napoleon's day—and was even styled after the Bastille. In the dirty, cramped cell, I could lie on my cot and touch both walls. The toilet was a covered pail; I don't care how strong you are, you can't stand having to smell a whole cell row of defecation."[1] (After the infamous "Cherry Hill" prison riot, the facility was permanently closed in 1955.[2])

In 1948, after a brief stint at Concord Prison, Malcolm (with the help of his sister Ella Collins) was transferred to Norfolk Prison, which was known for its focus on rehabilitation. Compared to Charlestown or Concord, Malcolm regarded Norfolk as "a heaven": "It had flushing toilets; there were no bars, only walls—and within the walls, you had far more freedom."[3] He also noted that each prisoner had their own room, had access to a large library, and was permitted visitors every day; and that professors from Harvard and other area colleges participated in the prison's educational programs.

When faced with descriptions of prisons like Charlestown or having been imprisoned in such repulsive places, many abolitionists have no doubt been inspired to dismantle the prison system. But while reformers too are inspired by such descriptions and experiences, they are moved to improve the practice rather than end it. Because prison conditions vary and some prisons are better than others, to decide whether to be a reformer or an abolitionist, it is necessary to know what a "prison" is and not just what some prisons are like. We need to identify which features of prisons are necessary characteristics (the elements that make a prison a prison), and which features are merely contingent and thus can be discarded or altered without dismantling the prison system entirely. I won't pretend that there is some ideologically neutral conception of a prison. Nor do I aim to provide a conception of the "ideal" prison. But I hope to offer a conception that reformers and abolitionists can accept, so that the disagreement turns, not on contentious or question-begging definitions, but on whether the familiar practice of imprisonment is one that, on moral or political grounds, should be abandoned.

To incarcerate is to subject a person to institutional confinement. Imprisonment, and thus "prison," is a type of incarceration. Incarceration, broadly conceived, has at least five elements. It entails *involuntary confinement*—restriction to a limited space with no right to leave without permission from authorities. This socio-spatial site of confinement is an *enclosed space* with a physically secure perimeter—walls, fences, locks, and guards—to prevent escape and unauthorized entry. Incarceration is not just a building with people locked inside. It is a *hierarchical institutional practice* defined by a set of rules, roles, and goals. These rules and roles vary with the overall justificatory aims of the institution (and sometimes with the covert purposes of its officials). Persons confined to carceral spaces are *isolated from the general public*—separated from others in the outside world (and sometimes from one another) and with highly restricted (if any) rights to visitation and to communicate with those outside (and sometimes within) the facility.

Importantly, these confined persons are in the *custody* of carceral authorities. Custody is a form of guardianship, which includes providing shelter, basic necessities, physical care, and protection from harm (including self-harm). If the incarcerated person is a known danger to others or to themselves, then they must sometimes be deprived of items that could inflict grave bodily harm. Providing adequate care and protection will sometimes require surveillance, searches, the enforcement of rules of order, or periods of confinement in a cell.[4]

Incarceration, so understood, can be used for a variety of purposes. Some of these purposes are legitimate: for instance, incarceration can be used to quarantine those with highly infectious and deadly diseases or to hold enemy combatants in times of war. Some uses of incarceration are clearly illegitimate: to keep a population available for exploitation, to repress political dissent, to torture people, or to use them for medical experiments.

Even within the context of crime control, incarceration can have several purposes. For example, there is pretrial detention. Such detention raises several issues for the reform-versus-abolition question. But I will leave these aside until later (Chapter 4). For now, my focus will be incarceration when its official purpose is *punishment*—a penalty for committing a crime. Indeed, Davis uses the phrase "punitive incarceration" to differentiate it from incarceration as detention while the prisoner awaits trial or a hearing.[5] In this book, I leave aside the complex issue of carceral detention for unlawful immigration or border crossing and its relationship to abolition.[6] This issue depends on resolving the challenging question of whether national borders should be enforced, controlled, or even exist, which I am not prepared to address here.[7]

An incarceration facility whose primary purpose is pretrial detention is a *jail*. We can call an incarceration facility whose primary purpose is prisoner rehabilitation a *penitentiary*. An incarceration facility that aims to treat and house those who suffer from serious psychological disorders is a *psychiatric hospital*. An incarceration facility that functions to impose punishment is a *prison*. These aims—detention, rehabilitation, treatment, and punishment—can be, and often are, combined within the same facility. Davis and other abolitionists oppose jails, penitentiaries, and prisons. So, for simplicity, I will refer to all three practices as "imprisonment" or simply "prison."

According to Davis, in the pre-modern era, before the emergence of capitalism and the nation-state, punishment was almost entirely *corporal*, from beatings to execution.[8] It is only with the rise of the bourgeois state that we get the general practice of punishment through incarceration: "Before the acceptance of the sanctity of individual rights, imprisonment could not have been understood as punishment. If the individual was not perceived as possessing inalienable rights and liberties, then the alienation of those rights and liberties by removal from society to a space tyrannically governed by the state would not have made sense."[9] I am not convinced that this historical claim is entirely accurate.[10] Regardless, if the debate between reformers and abolitionists is to be a meaningful one, this way of thinking about punishment and its relation to incarceration has limitations.

I suggest that punishment, whatever form it takes, be understood as unwelcome and unpleasant treatment. Such "hard treatment," as it is sometimes called, includes deprivation (whether of liberty, money, property, privileges, human contact, or life itself) as well as involuntary labor, public censure, humiliation, and so on. This definition is neutral between a range of justifications of punishment, including retribution and crime prevention. The hard-treatment conception of punishment is both narrower and broader than Davis's conception of punishment. It is narrower in that imprisonment as penalty need not imply that prisoners have forfeited all their rights thus permitting tyrannical treatment. If imprisonment entails that prisoners are rightless subjects under despotic rule, then prisons, at least in the United States, have already been abolished, as prisoners have many recognized rights—though not nearly all to which they are entitled.[11]

The conception of punishment I am suggesting is broader in that the forms of penalty need not be conceived as the deprivation of rights. Contrary to what Davis suggests, a conception of individuals as rights-bearers is not necessary for incarceration as punishment to make sense. Being held in a prison and subject to its rules would be regarded by almost anyone as deeply unpleasant and something to be avoided and so can serve as a deterrent or as retribution regardless of whether there is public recognition of individual rights. Prison also separates prisoners (if only temporarily) from their community and so functions similarly to banishment, which certainly existed in premodern eras. So I will operate with this broader conception of punishment—unwelcome and unpleasant treatment as penalty for a criminal offence.

A word about *incapacitation* through incarceration. It is, unfortunately, sometimes necessary to rely on incarceration to incapacitate highly dangerous individuals. There is a conceptual and a moral difference between incarcerating persons to prevent them from harming others (by restricting their movement to a highly limited and enclosed space) and incarcerating persons to penalize them for harmful actions they have already taken. Yet when carceral incapacitation is imposed in response to a criminal offense, it is practically indistinguishable from punishment. The same can be said when carceral incapacitation of a criminal offender is combined with rehabilitation or psychiatric treatment. These are all ways of using incarceration to respond to crime, where the hard treatment is triggered by and takes place only after a criminal offense. The same cannot be said of carceral incapacitation when it is used for the quarantine of those with deadly communicable diseases, for the involuntary commitment of mentally ill patients who have not perpetrated crimes, or for the confinement of enemy combatants in wartime. These incarcerated persons are regarded as dangerous enough to justify confining them, but their confinement is not punishment or even akin to punishment.

It is not possible to settle the reform-versus-abolition question without some engagement with the debate over the justification of punishment as such. What, if anything, justifies penalizing someone for breaking the law? I won't pursue this question in depth, as there is a vast philosophical literature on the subject, with intricacies that don't bear directly on our question.[12] But a few remarks are in order.

Davis does not regard *retribution* as a sound justification for punishment. That is, she does not think that the public has a right to seek revenge or to retaliate against those who break the law. She does not believe that those who do wrong, even serious wrong, "deserve" to suffer; nor does she accept that a criminal offender's misery has intrinsic value or could be in itself justice. She denies that people should suffer in proportion to the suffering they have wrongfully caused. The idea that bad people deserve prison is, she maintains, an ideological or sectarian notion.[13] As such, it is unsuitable as a public justification for coercion or confinement in a democratic society. Retributivism is a complex doctrine, with many variants. It also has undeniable intuitive appeal to many and is consonant with widely held religious views. Nevertheless, I am largely in agreement with Davis in not accepting retributive justifications of punishment, though I will not defend this stance in the present book. Nothing I say here about "punishment" or "penalties" should be construed as endorsing retributive ideas.

Yet, while these objections pose obstacles for retributive defenses of punishment, they do not stand in the way of punishment when it is used as a method for preventing or reducing crime. Penalizing crime through incarceration is plausibly and widely viewed as an effective and fair way to prevent and control criminal wrongdoing—as a means for a society to provide a reasonable level of security for our persons, liberties, and rightful possessions. Retribution or retaliation need not be part of incarceration's aim. Unless abolitionists equate all punishment with retribution, they are best understood as claiming (among other things) that the need to prevent and control crime is an inadequate justification for the use of prisons.

I regard imprisonment as justified only if milder penalties are insufficient to control crime adequately. As with self-defense and just war measures, we should cause no more suffering than is necessary to protect people from harmful wrongdoing. Prisons should also not be used unless there are good reasons to believe they help to prevent crime (an issue I will address in Chapter 5). Prisons would indeed be obsolete—and immoral—if they are unnecessary or incapable of reducing crime.

I also agree with Davis that incarceration should not be the primary method for preventing crime. Imposing a prison sentence should not be the first answer nor the default response to criminal wrongdoing. Less harmful alternatives should be considered and prioritized, relying on prisons as a last resort. Moreover, much crime is a symptom of underlying structural injustices that demand redress, and thus some crime could be prevented by creating more just social conditions. I also agree with Davis therefore that many societies—and especially the United States—grossly *overuse* punitive incarceration. Even under more just circumstances than prevail in the United States, I would favor using fines and property confiscation, community service and other work assignments, restitution and reparation, electronic monitoring, home confinement, supervised probation, and the loss of certain privileges (for example, suspension of driver's license) for most criminal offenses.[14] Incarceration is a drastic crime-control measure, best reserved for the most serious offenses and for those offenders who, even after suffering less severe penalties, continue to show disregard for others' basic rights.

By "the most serious crimes," I mean offenses that do great and irreparable harm or crimes that cause deep and lasting trauma, such as homicide, rape, and aggravated assault. Major white-collar or corporate crime can sometimes cause immense harms that can't be repaired. Misdemeanors, though sometimes punished with short prison sentences, are not serious crimes. Not all felonies—legally prohibited actions punishable by more than a year of incarceration—count as "the most serious" on my account either. For instance, many property crimes (auto theft, burglary, and larceny) and some types of fraud (credit-card fraud, passing bad checks, and forgery) are considered felonies in the United States but generally do not cause great and irreparable harm or lasting trauma. A similar thing could be said about some drug offenses and the illegal possession of firearms. Perhaps under some circumstances, imprisonment can be justifiably used to penalize these less serious offenses. But if we find that imprisonment is legitimately used to prevent the most serious crimes, then that would go a long way toward showing that prison reform remains an appropriate goal.

Few would deny that actions that are wrong and cause harm should sometimes be penalized to reduce the incidence of such actions. Inexcusable harmful wrongdoing should have "consequences," where these consequences involve some unwelcome and unpleasant treatment. Otherwise, many who commit such acts are likely to repeat them; and others, noticing that these acts have been undertaken without negative consequence, will be encouraged to engage in similar acts themselves. Consider speeding and other reckless driving, which leads to thousands of deaths and serious injuries each year in the United States. Abolitionists need not reject *all* punishments as unjustified. A world where no action incurs a penalty is not the demand. They simply deny that incarceration is among the permissible punishments for wrongdoing.

So why prison? After all, there are less harmful penalties available. I think the first thing to say is that imprisonment is likely the harshest penalty a society can impose that also plausibly satisfies human rights requirements. Some penalties, though still used in a few places, are too harsh and inhumane, for example, maiming and death. No one should be subjected to these, even for serious wrongdoing. Other penalties are too mild to deter serious crimes. A fine or community service is unlikely to be severe enough to discourage murder or rape.

Another reason prison could sometimes be the right kind of penalty is that there is on occasion a need to protect the vulnerable from imminent harm. Imprisonment is a way of temporarily incapacitating a dangerous individual. Other penalties prevent crime primarily by way of deterrence, a threat which some will inevitably fail to heed. Home confinement comes closest to incapacitation. But here, the perimeter of the residence is not secure, so the offender could leave the home (even if electronically monitored) and anyone could enter. Such confinement provides only limited protection for those outside or inside the home. It is true, imprisonment cannot completely prevent a prisoner from harming others (for instance, fellow prisoners, prison staff, or visitors), and occasionally prisoners escape. But the personnel, physical structure, and rules of a prison can provide greater security from imminent attack than any viable and nonlethal alternative.

During the period of institutional confinement, a prisoner might learn to better control their antisocial impulses or to change the habits of mind that led them to harm others. The isolation and structure of prison can be an opportunity for serious reflection, a chance to reconsider how one should live and relate to others, which the prisoner may not have done otherwise or even realized they needed to do. If suitably staffed and organized, prison can be a space for rehabilitation, which is itself a way to prevent and control crime, as most prisoners are, in time, released back into the public.

Given these considerations—that is, the possible effectiveness of carceral deterrence, incapacitation, and rehabilitation—it is easy to see how a people, concerned to protect the basic rights of its members, might adopt the practice of imprisonment without being motivated by malice, vengeance, cruelty, or greed. Prisons hold out the promise that harmful wrongdoing can be controlled with minimal violence and that prisoners, after rehabilitation, can eventually rejoin the community on equal terms. Unlike with the deadly harm and destruction traded between nations at war, a people would naturally be reluctant to resort to lethal force when dealing with the unjust aggression of its own members, provided a suitable alternative was available.

Some naturally look upon prisons in horror. To contemplate being locked inside a prison cell or an enclosed facility is the stuff of nightmares. It is not at all surprising many have come to think that only a diabolical mind could have dreamed up such an institution. Yet, without denying the terrifying prospect that a prison sentence represents, I believe it is understandable why a people might use prisons to reduce crime in its midst, particularly once the penalties of exile, torture, maiming, and death have been repudiated as immoral. Imprisonment may nonetheless be an objectionable punitive practice for the reasons abolitionists cite. Let's turn now to those objections.

Dehumanization, Agency, and Preventative Force

The imprisonment of humans is often likened to the caging and torturing of animals. Prisons are thought to impose prolonged discomfort and daily torment. Some abolitionists believe that by virtue of being incarcerated, prisoners are marked as less than fully human or are treated in ways that no human should be. They maintain, in other words, that imprisonment is incompatible with basic human dignity. This position is different from claiming that dehumanizing and inhumane practices exist in many prisons, particularly American prisons, a claim that many reformers would strongly endorse. Not all these troubling practices are essential to punitive incarceration—for example, routine and invasive strip searches; using prisoner numbers (instead of given names) when directly addressing incarcerated persons; requiring humiliating and stigmatizing prisoner uniforms; or discussing prisoners as if they were subhuman or animals in need of taming. Ending these and similar practices would not constitute abolishing prisons, only reforming them.

Davis sometimes cites dehumanizing and inhumane aspects to existing prison practices that reformers are, and have long been, at pains to change. Many of these changes are clearly feasible, because they have already been instituted in some prison systems around the world (for instance, in prisons in Norway, the Netherlands, and Germany) and in some U.S. states.[15] These changes include increasing the standard size of prison cells; limiting cells to one occupant to enable greater privacy; eliminating facility overcrowding; providing proper ventilation, heating, and cooling; ensuring regular access to natural light and fresh air; requiring thorough screening and extensive training for prison staff; increasing staff levels to avoid reliance on gangs and routinization to ensure order; providing high quality and essential medical care (physical and mental); maintaining sanitation and a healthy physical environment to prevent illness, the spread of disease, and pest infestation; prohibiting the shackling of prisoners while they are in labor or giving birth; allowing persons who have recently given birth to be housed with their newborns to enable proper bonding; facilitating frequent interaction and communication between prisoners; permitting regular phone calls to and visits from family and friends; ensuring adequate nutrition and opportunities for exercise and recreation; providing supplies for personal hygiene; facilitating religious observance and honoring religious freedom; maintaining a well-stocked and wide-ranging library; and protecting prisoners from prisoner and guard violence, including sexual assault. A number of these conditions are not met in supermaximum-security facilities, which is why many reformers oppose them on human rights grounds.[16] There is also broad opposition to extended periods in solitary confinement, which is arguably a form of torture and sometimes causes irreparable psychological harm.[17]

Human beings are like other animals in many ways. We share several welfare interests with them. Yet, unlike other animals, we do not act merely from instinct, impulse, or habit. We have the capacity to consciously reflect on possible courses of action and to successfully resist the temptation to act on urges, even powerful ones. We are also capable of deliberately treating others either justly or unjustly, with kindness or cruelty. Not mere possible recipients of just and humane treatment, we have the capacity to accord others the respect and treatment they are owed. No creature should be made to suffer needlessly or regarded as lacking all value. But as creatures capable of rationality and agency, of reasoned deliberation and conscious choice, human beings are to be treated in a way that honors our status as rational agents, as *persons* and not merely as animals.

Imprisonment, even if humane, might therefore be deemed inherently dehumanizing insofar as it fails to respect prisoners' status as persons.

To respond to abolitionist concerns, reformers must explain how imprisonment, despite the deprivation and suffering it inevitably imposes on prisoners, is compatible with respect for persons as free and rational.[18] They should also make clear that they have a realistic and nonideological conception of human agency such that it is fair to sometimes impose prison as a penalty for serious crimes. And reformers need to show that the interests protected by using imprisonment are sufficiently weighty to justify such a severe crime-control measure.

Human beings should not be treated as if they were mere objects to be manipulated for this or that purpose, even when the purpose is a worthy one (for example, public safety). To regard someone as an agent—and so to accord them the dignity they are due as a human being—is to view them as capable of rational deliberation and choice. To respect this agency, we should appeal to others through reasons. In the practical realm, there are *moral* and *prudential* reasons. We offer moral reasons to others when we draw their attention to a valid moral consideration (say, that murder needlessly ends a life of inherent and irreplaceable value), which some may nevertheless discount or ignore. We offer prudential reasons when we make others aware of how a course of action could diminish their own well-being or cause them harm. A threat, say, a warning of a pending legal sanction, provides a prudential reason, which the targeted person can choose whether to heed. Criminal laws, when just, provide both kinds of reasons—a morally grounded prohibition and a sanction for noncompliance.

The requirement to refrain from using physical violence (except in self-defense, in defense of others from imminent attack, or in a just war) is a moral duty that almost any adult (and many children) can be expected to know they have and to comply with. Parents, teachers, and religious leaders instruct youth to conduct themselves nonviolently and to avoid needlessly harming others. The law codifies this duty when it prohibits murder, rape, robbery, and assault. With some crimes, such as a violent act that required planning, and which thus the perpetrator had time to reconsider carrying it out, we confront an especially grave wrong that warrants an appropriate, even coercive, response. It is such manifest unwillingness to respect others' right to be free from physical aggression that sometimes justifies our resorting to credible threats (negative incentives) to prevent wrongful harms.

Those greatly burdened by social injustices (and, at times, their more privileged allies) will sometimes justifiably break the law and evade law enforcement. They may do so for reasons of pressing economic need, self-defense against illegitimate state violence, or political resistance. The psychological and social pressures of oppression can make it difficult to remain within legal bounds while also maintaining one's dignity; or these pressures may compel or tempt one to break the law for completely understandable or even excusable reasons (for example, because of reasonable anger or the need for catharsis). Some of what is generally considered "crime" may be activities that no state should prohibit or punish (for instance, some drug use or sex work).

Matters are different with the kinds of serious wrongs I have in mind. The moral considerations against murder and rape, for example, provide sufficient and overriding reasons to refrain from these egregious wrongs, which cause great and irreparable harm and severe trauma. The fact that a person is oppressed can neither override these reasons nor render them inapplicable. The need to protect the vulnerable, including many who are themselves oppressed, is what justifies penalizing these grave wrongs through incarceration.

There is of course a weighty moral proscription against subjecting others to physical force and confinement. But this proscription is conditional. It depends on a person not acting in an unjustly aggressive way toward others. Those who wrong others in ways that typically cause great harm cannot reasonably object to the unpleasant and coercive treatment their own wrongful conduct has called forth, provided such treatment is necessary to prevent harm to others.

This use of hard treatment, a form of preventative force, is neither dehumanizing nor unfair, at least not when prisons are humane and courts operate justly. Forewarned by the public legal proscription and equipped with the capacity for rational and free action, offenders had an adequate opportunity to avoid this unwelcome and unpleasant treatment. They could have refrained from serious wrongdoing but chose not to. They, through their own willful actions, have created a situation where others are morally permitted to take strong measures against them to avoid grave harm to themselves. It is this problem of wrongful aggression, an unfortunate reality of human social relations, that generates the necessity for a proportional response to thwart the threat of harm.

What I am identifying are the moral permissions and constraints on getting others to do things they already have overriding reasons to do but at times refuse to. When people refuse to

listen to moral reasons, we are sometimes permitted to use coercive means to alter their behavior, particularly when we or
others would otherwise be gravely harmed. But their refusal to
listen does not mean that the state no longer has a responsibility
to respect their rights or that they have somehow surrendered
their right to just and humane treatment. In protecting the vulnerable from the unjust aggression of others, the state should
honor as many of the aggressor's ordinary rights as is compatible with securing people against harmful wrongdoing.[19]

Now, some persons are not so much unwilling as *incapable*
of recognizing and responding appropriately to moral or prudential reasons. This could be due to youth, cognitive or emotional
disorders, developmental impairment, or mental illness. The
rational agency of these persons is so underdeveloped, dimin-
ished, or compromised that it would be wrong and pointless to
hold them accountable for their wrongful acts. These persons
require treatment, care, and support but not punitive action. If
they must be temporarily confined and isolated to prevent harm
to others or self-harm, this should be in a mental-health facility,
not a prison.

Such involuntary confinement to a psychiatric hospital,
though not punishment, is *incarceration*—the institutionalized
practice of forcibly confining people within an enclosed space,
segregating them from the general public, claiming custodial
guardianship over them, and subjecting them to institutional
rules of order. The same is true of the involuntary quarantine of
those with extremely deadly communicable diseases and the
confinement of captured enemy combatants in a war. And so if
these modes of incarceration are, at least sometimes, morally
permissible (and I think they are), incarceration *as such* cannot

be inherently dehumanizing, at least not if all dehumanization is immoral treatment and a violation of human rights.[20] The problem would have to be with certain uses, purposes, or functions of incarceration.

Abolitionists could object that this account of agency exaggerates humans' capacity for moral and rational action or that it fails to appreciate how the agency of the oppressed has been compromised by the structural violence of unjust institutions. They might add that prisons are filled with unjustly disadvantaged people who have themselves been victims of serious wrongs (for example, sexual assault or child abuse), sometimes the same wrongs they have committed, and that this victimization and trauma can explain their moral failures and trouble with the law. Treatment, not punishment, it could be argued, is the appropriate response to their harmful conduct.

Davis says, however, that she is not against holding individuals, even deeply disadvantaged persons, accountable for their harmful acts.[21] Skepticism about the agency of those who themselves have been victims is not, in any case, something Davis could consistently endorse, as she calls for social movements centered on achieving justice; and this call presupposes that human beings, including those who are oppressed, are ordinarily capable of recognizing and acting on considerations of justice. A purely rehabilitative or therapeutic approach to crime fits uneasily with a conception of the oppressed as agents of radical social change whose defiance of law is sometimes a conscious act of political resistance. Prisoners, on Davis's account, do typically possess and exercise agency in the sense described here (see Chapter 1). Indeed, a stable and just social order would be impossible if there were no feasible circumstances under which individuals could, by and large, be expected to comply with what justice demands despite sometimes being tempted or inclined to do otherwise.

Some abolitionists claim that the state dehumanizes those within its territorial jurisdiction when it uses violence (or the threat of violence) against these persons, even when it does so to prevent wrongful violence.[22] Yet it is hard to consistently maintain that ordinary citizens are permitted to engage in defensive harm to protect themselves or others from wrongful aggression but insist that state officials are never permitted to use force to reduce the incidence of murder or rape. Indeed, many radical abolitionists believe that revolutionary violence is sometimes justified, whether in the struggle against capitalism and fascism or in national liberation movements against colonialism. Among abolitionists who might disapprove of violent social revolution, many still celebrate slave revolts and defend the right of armed self-defense against illegitimate state violence. Presumably, such actions, though violent, are not dehumanizing.

There is also the commitment of abolition feminists and organizations like Survived & Punished to defend criminalized survivors of gender and sexual violence.[23] Consider the famous case of Joanne ("Joan") Little.[24] On August 27, 1974, Little was being held at Beaufort County Jail in North Carolina on charges of breaking and entering when Clarence Alligood, a jail officer, entered her cell with an ice pick hoping to compel Little into sex. Little managed to stab Alligood with the ice pick (some eleven times) and escaped from the jail. Alligood died from his wounds. After a highly publicized weeklong law-enforcement hunt, Little surrendered and was charged with first-degree murder. Little claimed she had acted in self-defense against attempted rape. Many noted black leaders and artists strongly supported her, and a "Free Joan Little" movement emerged, with hundreds of supporters rallying outside the courthouse during her trial. In fact, in a June 1975 article for *Ms. Magazine*, Angela Davis defended Little's actions as a courageous act of self-defense and resistance to sexual assault in prison.[25] After hearing testimony from Little and from other black women survivors of Alligood's sexual assaults, a jury acquitted Little of the murder charges. I doubt that many abolitionists would claim that Little's violent actions in self-defense dehumanized Alligood.

The only way to coherently affirm that revolutionary violence, slave rebellion, or violence in self-defense is sometimes permitted but that state violence is always illegitimate is to defend anarchism—to argue that no state has the authority to use physical coercion or intentional harm to enforce laws because a state, no matter how fairly or benevolently it operated, could never have a rightful claim on others' obedience to its laws.[26] Anarchists deny that state-legal authority (and sometimes any hierarchical social organization) is ever legitimate, and accordingly many oppose *all* state sanctions for lawbreaking, not just incarceration. There are anarchists who are also prison abolitionists.[27]

Yet anarchist commitments don't necessarily rule out the use of incarceration to prevent or reduce serious wrongdoing. Charges of wrongdoing, trials, and punishment can, and do, occur in communities that are not organized as states, as with many pre-modern traditional societies. This kind of treatment, an anarchist might allow, is the province of stateless communities, as opposed to an exclusive prerogative of territorially sovereign states (here understood in the Westphalian sense). A self-governing (though non-state) community could come to consensus that the practice of imprisonment is the most effective, most humane, and fairest way to limit serious wrongs and thereby maintain a flourishing community.

Prison reformers generally accept that it is sometimes necessary and justifiable to use harm to prevent harm. Some abolitionists, however, reject the use of harm to address harm. The pacifist abolitionist (who might also be an anarchist) thus does have a consistent position on the use of harm. Some pacifists do not merely oppose killing, state violence, and war but are against all violence and coercion. Therefore, it is easy for them to explain why they abhor and reject prisons. Imprisonment, as a form of involuntary confinement that curtails prisoners' basic liberties, necessarily involves the use of force and the intentional imposition of harm. It is a violent practice. The challenge for pacifists is to explain convincingly why there is a duty to abstain from violence even when we are wrongly threatened by it and even when aggressors will not otherwise be contained or deterred.

I doubt we have a duty to absorb or submit to the harm that others wrongly seek to inflict upon us. I also doubt we have a duty to always choose flight or supplication when violently threatened. It would take a lot to persuade me that harming others, particularly when the harm is nonlethal, is *always* unjustified. To be sure, pacifism raises interesting philosophical questions about the political morality of nonviolence. I won't explore them further, though. A pacifist abolitionism is not the form of abolition that I find most challenging or compelling. And Davis does not use pacifism as a premise in her arguments against prisons. Indeed, the form of black radicalism from which Davis's anti-prison activism initially emerged, and for which I have much sympathy, positioned itself in stark opposition to the mainstream Civil Rights movement's commitment to rely solely on nonviolent resistance to fight injustice (see Chapter 1).

Imprisonment as Slavery

As we saw in Chapter 1, many influential black radical thinkers— George Jackson, Huey Newton, and Assata Shakur—have compared prison to enslavement. Davis herself maintains that "slavery continues to live on in contemporary institutions—as in the cases of the death penalty and the prison."[28] She states that there is "a clear relationship between the rise of the prison-industrial-complex in the era of global capitalism and the persistence of structures in the punishment system that originated with slavery."[29] Davis tells us that because new democratic institutions were not developed to end the conditions that created American slavery, "black people encountered new forms of slavery—from debt peonage and the convict lease system to segregated and second-class education. The prison system continues to carry out this terrible legacy."[30] Perhaps most famously, she claims, "obvious vestiges of enslavement persist within the U.S. prison system. The Thirteenth Amendment [to the U.S. Constitution] abolished slavery for all except those who have been convicted of a crime. That is why many of us have suggested that we need a modern-day abolitionist movement."[31]

If the practice of imprisonment is akin to slavery, then prison abolition would naturally be an urgent and necessary response for all who care about justice. The two institutions—slavery and imprisonment—are strikingly similar and have sometimes been combined. Enslaved Africans, for example, were imprisoned throughout their terrifying and deadly journey across the Atlantic during the Middle Passage. Slavery can and has taken place in the context of incarceration, as with the post–Civil War convict-leasing system in the United States.[32] And the threat of incarceration has been used to perpetuate slavery or slave-like conditions. Yet there *are* differences between enslavement and imprisonment that are morally relevant to assessing the legitimacy of incarceration as punishment.

Before getting to those differences, we should pause again to register that the thesis that imprisonment is a kind of slavery is extremely radical, particularly if the paradigm for slavery is the chattel slavery that Africans and peoples of African descent experienced in the Americas. And the charge that prison is legalized slavery, if true, would have far-reaching practical implications. Slavery, understood as absolute despotism, puts the enslaved and their captors in a state of war. This kind of abject oppression, particularly when it endures over a long period, is widely thought to license the use of political violence and to void the authority of laws that permit and facilitate the practice and perhaps to invalidate the entire legal order and governing regime. For instance, the slave rebellion in Saint-Domingue and the revolutionary struggle to found Haiti as an independent nation were premised on this moral foundation.[33] Of course, the fact that a moral or political position is radical or calls for drastic action does not show that the position is incorrect. Nevertheless, we should keep the radical implications of the critique in mind as we assess its soundness and consider alternatives.

There is no doubt that slavery is a powerful and enduring symbol in black political culture. The historical memory of enslavement has profoundly shaped black identities and continues to have deep emotional resonance among black peoples. In addition, fugitive slaves and slave revolts are generally venerated as heroic in black political culture.[34] It is therefore not surprising that prison abolitionists in the black radical tradition regularly invoke slavery and slave resistance when seeking to mobilize people, particularly African Americans, in anti-prison initiatives. But my aim is not to assess whether narratives about slavery and its similarity to imprisonment are effective means for inspiring political action. Rhetorical strategy, though obviously important, is not my primary interest in abolition. I am concerned with invocations of slavery in contemporary social criticism, and seek to determine whether the *substance* of this form of criticism is valid, and if so, how it bears on the disagreement between reformers and abolitionists.

Within some systems of slavery, slaveholders have (near) absolute power over their slaves. This dominion includes complete control over the body and activities of the slave, sometimes extending to the discretion to determine whether the enslaved will live or die. However, when a state's power over prisoners is legitimate, it is not arbitrary despotic power. Human rights requirements, constitutional restrictions, and the democratic authority of legislative bodies properly limit the state's power to control and shape the lives of prisoners. Imprisonment cannot be permissibly imposed without satisfying due process requirements—just searches, freedom from coerced confessions, habeas corpus, rights to defend oneself against charges, access to legal counsel, impartial trials, fair sentences, opportunities to appeal court judgments, and so on.

Moreover, it is not a necessary feature of imprisonment that prisoners are sold, leased out, or used as collateral in commercial deals. Ending the practice of commodifying prisoners does not require the abolition of prisons as such. Institutionalized custodial confinement need not entail that the state has property rights over a prisoner's body or labor. Nor does claiming that incarceration is sometimes legitimate imply that prison officials are permitted to use torture or corporal punishment to force prisoners to work or to ensure labor discipline.

It is true that locks, physical restraints, and guards are used to prevent prisoners from escaping. But coercive measures to prevent escape are sometimes justified, as with extremely violent patients in psychiatric hospitals or with prisoners of war. All forms of incarceration, whether or not punishment is the aim, entail significant interference with the basic liberties of those confined (freedom of movement, association, privacy, and so on).

Since enslavement and imprisonment often involve involuntary labor, the slave/prisoner analogy may seem more promising if work under coercive conditions is highlighted. Yet we should distinguish between forced labor as an indefinite or permanent condition (which is typical of slavery), and a specified and limited period of involuntary labor, as might be imposed as part of a prison sentence. The scope of the involuntary labor might also be restricted to a specific, perhaps even narrow, range of activities, and excluding things like the coerced provision of sexual services or other degrading activities. When the timeframe for and range of activities is thus limited, it is not obvious to me why prison labor couldn't be a legitimate penalty for serious crimes. Some who are convicted of lesser crimes are sentenced to periods of community service or assigned specific labor tasks. This labor is not voluntary either, but its imposition can sometimes be justified.

The objection to prison labor cannot be that it combines two different types of penalty—incarceration and involuntary labor. After all, monetary fines and prison terms are sometimes combined, as are financial restitution and community service. I cannot see what principled reason there could be for forbidding such mixed penalties, provided they are proportionate to the crime and could help reduce crime overall.

Assume that an explicit period of imprisonment (for instance, seven years) is a morally permissible and proportionate penalty for certain crimes (say, attempted murder). Also suppose that limited work assignments are a legitimate punishment for criminal wrongdoing. If these assumptions hold, then it seems to me that offering a *shorter* prison term on the condition that the convicted offender work during the period of confinement is sometimes permissible. The same thing happens when community service is offered as an alternative punishment to a justified prison sentence. The reasonable assumption here is that if an offender chooses a sentence that includes prison labor over a longer prison sentence that lacks a work component, then they must regard the first as less severe.

There is a powerful counterexample to the claim that it is morally acceptable to offer a shorter prison sentence if the offender accepts work penalties. If the offer of a shorter sentence included a condition that the offender be sterilized, that would clearly be objectionable even if the offender were to accept it. In May 2017, Tennessee Judge Sam Benningfield signed a controversial court order permitting prisoners in the White County jail to receive thirty days off their sentence if they allowed themselves to be sterilized, and several imprisoned women and men agreed to the arrangement.[35] This outrageous "offer" might lead one to conclude that so-called alternative penalties are always unjust because they are *coercive*. Once incarceration is the sentence (particularly when the sentence is long), we can expect some convicted persons to do almost anything, even self-mortification or degrading acts, to reduce their prison time.

On the other hand, if the offer of a shorter sentence included a condition that the prisoner regularly see a psychotherapist, undergo treatment for a drug use disorder, or participate in vocational training, this strikes me as much more acceptable. Perhaps this is because these alternative penalties (though maybe initially regarded as unwelcome by the prisoner) could help the imprisoned person, at least in the long run. This is a good reason to ensure involuntary prison labor benefits prisoners in some way other than simply shortening their time in prison. They could, at least upon reflection or in retrospect, come to endorse the value of such work.

Not only could sterilization irreparably harm prisoners; it would, if not freely chosen, wrongly interfere with their reproductive freedom. Perhaps another lesson of the counterexample is that the alternative sentence must take the form of a penalty that the state has the authority to impose. Sterilization cannot be a legitimate penalty, whether taken alone or added to a prison term. But a limited work assignment could be, as for example with community service.

Compelled community service and prison labor can be justified on grounds of deterrence and rehabilitation. Both forms of work are typically disagreeable, are not freely chosen, and are generally regarded as burdensome. Therefore, the threat of their imposition can serve as an incentive to avoid breaking the law. Involuntary labor, when it is of the right sort, could also instill discipline, useful skills, cooperative habits, and self-esteem. This moral reform could thus reduce the likelihood that the prisoner, once released, will commit further crimes.

Some abolitionists might accept that prison labor that serves the common good in a just society is permissible. Yet they might object, not so much to the fact that prison labor is involuntary, but to the fact that such compelled work would be performed under the dominion and for the purposes of a *private will*—a corporate power, rather than a public one. Coerced privatized prison labor—particularly when done for corporate profit—arguably makes such work a form of involuntary *servitude*. We each have a basic interest in having the freedom to abstain from working for companies that produce goods and services we strongly disapprove of or that have practices (including labor practices) we object to. We should not be forced to submit to the arbitrary commands or to serve the private ends of another.

We do not, however, have a similar liberty with respect to public service, as we can justifiably be required to provide, say, military service and jury duty, at least when the background social structure is just and the governing regime legitimate. Here we would be submitting to the public will under the rule of law, and our efforts would contribute to maintaining the just social order from which we benefit. If the goods and services produced through prison labor were used by other state agencies in the provision of public goods, this could not be reasonably construed as involuntary servitude. Moreover, requiring prisoners to contribute labor that serves the public good would be one way for them to repair the civic bonds that have been frayed due to their criminal conduct. It could pave the way for reconciliation with their fellow citizens.

It could be objected that prison laborers are denied freedom of occupational choice, as they are usually assigned their tasks or must choose among a narrow range of options. Prisoners also typically lack a recognized right to organize, strike, and bargain for better work conditions. Perhaps these labor freedoms (like freedom of religion and freedom from torture) are liberties that cannot be curtailed even if one has committed a serious crime. So there might be a case that prison labor is unjust (if not a form of slavery).

The case would face some difficulties, though. The state, through imprisonment alone, would be interfering with what appear to be even more fundamental liberties—freedom of movement, association, privacy, and so on. But maybe this interference is necessary for crime control in a way that interfering with labor freedoms is not. In addition, a sentence of community service would also curtail labor rights but does not appear to be inherently unjust. Still, prison reformers could, and probably should, insist that incarcerated workers have legal counsel or chosen representatives (if not unions) to advocate and negotiate on their behalf regarding labor assignments, compensation, and work conditions.

But let's suppose it is always wrong to use prison labor to penalize legally prohibited wrongdoing. In a society that is otherwise just, would it also be unfair to require convicted prisoners to help reduce the costs of their room and board? I am not certain that it would be. It would not be unfair, for example, to expect prisoners to prepare their own food, clean up after themselves, and do their own laundry rather than have the public pay for these services to be provided at no cost to prisoners. This work is comparable to ordinary domestic labor. If this type of prison work does not run afoul of fairness, why would it be unfair to expect prisoners to also help defray the costs of their clothing and food by producing goods or providing services useful to public agencies? Even Marx allows that some of the work a wage laborer does is *necessary labor* (the work needed to meet the material needs of workers and their dependents). The capitalist, recall, only appropriates *surplus* labor—that is, the labor beyond necessary labor.

Incarcerating prisoners in a humane way is expensive and inevitably draws on public revenue that could be used for other purposes. When prisoners have dependents, the public might have to supplement the income of their families. And, arguably, all in society who are able should, on grounds of reciprocity or productive justice, contribute *something* to reproducing the social and material conditions that sustain our common life together.[36] So the requirement that prisoners work in some capacity is not, as such, unjust, even if work *as punishment* is.

Slaves are generally unpaid or paid very little. One could object, then, that prisoners forced to work are slaves insofar as they are not paid, not paid a market wage, or not paid a fair wage.[37] But suppose they were paid a market wage. This compensated labor would raise the already considerable costs to the public of taking care of prisoners' basic needs. Would state confiscation of a portion of these wages to defray the expense of incarceration be unfair? I am not sure that it would be. It would be comparable to a tax or to garnishing wages for an unpaid public debt.[38]

Nevertheless, there is little doubt that prisoners should receive higher wages than they typically do. (For instance, in no state in America are they paid anywhere close to the federal minimum wage, which is itself egregiously low.[39]) Yet better pay for prison labor would still be reform, not abolition. Or if better pay for prison labor does count as "abolition," then many reformers are abolitionists, and the call to abolish the prison turns out to be a moderate demand—which is not to say that it would be easy to secure it.

I would emphasize that the opportunity to work while in prison could be of considerable value to prisoners themselves, at least under current economic structures (for example, where there is an extensive labor market and no unconditional guaranteed basic income). It would give prisoners a chance to show that they are reliable workers and could help them establish an employment record during their period of confinement, which could improve their employment prospects once they are released. This work history could, in addition, be used to show that they are ready to be released, that they will be able to secure and keep a job and thus are less likely to turn to crime. The work itself gives prisoners something constructive to do. Unstructured prison life is intensely boring and monotonous, and too much prisoner idleness often leads to mischief and interpersonal conflict, which needlessly adds to the burdens of prison.

Imprisonment is extremely hard on the families of prisoners and often strains (and sometimes breaks) familial bonds. If prisoners have opportunities to earn money, they can financially assist their families, if only in small ways, and this can help to strengthen or repair family ties. A gift from an imprisoned parent can mean a lot to a child and reduces the shame prisoners sometimes feel for being unable to play a larger role in the care and raising of their children. Through paid work prisoners could also earn money to buy things they want (small creature comforts), which lessens the financial burden on their families. Or they could save some money to ease their reentry into society.

Moreover, when prison labor plays a key role in the maintenance and operation of the prison, this gives prisoners some leverage in bargaining for better working and prison conditions. They can then withdraw their labor in protest (or threaten to do so) and may thereby gain some concessions. Where all the necessary work is done by prison staff, prisoners have little power they can wield collectively (apart from, say, rioting or hunger strikes).

Generally, prisoners should be permitted to exercise as many of their basic liberties as are compatible with their prison sentence and the requirements of custodial care. This means allowing prisoners to exercise many of their political liberties and economic freedoms, as well as permitting them regular contact (through phone calls, letters, electronic communication, and in-person visits) with persons outside the prison where feasible. If we think of their penalty as hard treatment designed to control crime (through deterrence, rehabilitation, or incapacitation) rather than as civic death (the suspension of all their basic rights), exile (banishment from civil society), or retribution (imposing the suffering they deserve), then this makes perfect sense.

No reasonable person thinks that when offenders are penalized through fines or mandatory community service, they should also lose their social, civic, and economic freedoms. These freedoms are properly curtailed only insofar as this is necessary to impose or administer a just sentence. We could and should construe imprisonment similarly. So, for instance, facilitating and compensating prison work could be a way of respecting prisoners' right to work and earn money. Thus, prisoners should at least, where feasible, have the *option* (and perhaps be strongly encouraged) to work while incarcerated.[40]

What this series of reflections has revealed is that the practice of imprisonment is not, or at least need not be, a form of slavery (where enslavement is understood as inherently unjust). Yet the main problem with the slave labor/prisoner labor analogy is that someone convicted of a serious crime (unlike, say, a chattel slave) has been judged to have committed a grave wrong, and prison labor is the penalty for the transgression. If a person's crimes do not permit the state to curtail their liberties to control crime, then imprisonment, even without involuntary labor, is effectively *kidnapping*—the wrongful abduction and confinement of another against their will. Obviously, a state cannot permissibly punish someone—whether through imprisonment, involuntary labor, fines, property confiscation, or suspension of privileges—on the grounds that the person is a member of a stigmatized, disliked, or powerless social group. If it can justly punish at all, it can do so only in response to an unlawful act that is legitimately prohibited; and it can impose such penalties only on the person(s) who committed the act.

The abolitionist criticism that practices of imprisonment are continuous with slavery is most compelling when understood as a critique of some past or existing prisons. It is a forceful and appropriate moral condemnation of prisons as they once were and as some now are. Some prisons do share features with slavery that make them morally unacceptable. But it is not a powerful criticism when applied to all prisons or to prisons as they might be if suitably reformed. Nor does it help to resolve the reform-versus-abolition debate. The moral charge that prisons are slavery would justify abolition only if the practice of imprisonment could not exist without sharing objectionable features with the practice of enslavement.

Prisons as a Legacy of Slavery

Davis and like-minded abolitionists identify surprising *historical* relationships between enslavement and imprisonment. Different historical links can be postulated, and the practical significance of each link—for example, whether it points toward reform, demands abolition, or has no practical import—varies. I see this criticism as offering a *genealogical critique* of the prison, and consider several ways to understand the historical connection between enslavement and imprisonment.

Within the critical theory tradition, genealogical critique does not always aim to show that the practice being examined should be abandoned or replaced. It needn't imply the automatic rejection of the object of critique. The objective of the historical analysis can sometimes be to free us from a too-easy acceptance of the practice, from a complacent and unreflective endorsement of it.[41] The critical analysis often works by demonstrating the role of contingent power relations in the origins of the practice, which dissolves the sense of inevitability that surrounds it. The genealogical critique can free, if not radicalize, our imagination, empowering us to experiment with different ways of doing things or at least to consider new possibilities.

Many people, without giving the matter much thought, treat the practice of imprisonment as natural and inescapable, as a necessary feature of social life that has always been and thus will always be with us. Captive to this picture, they do not see the need to justify or scrutinize the prison. Genealogical critique can break the hold of this perspective (which many are unaware they are in the grip of), enabling us to take a more critical stance toward the practice and possibly leading us to make significant changes to it. I think we can read Michel Foucault's *Discipline and Punish: The Birth of the Prison* (1975) as offering a critique of this sort (though other interpretations are possible).

To the extent that Davis's genealogical critique of imprisonment (tracing the genesis of prisons to practices of enslavement) frees our imagination, encourages reevaluation, and prepares the way for arguments for prison abolition, I regard it as immensely valuable. We should not take the prison for granted or regard its justification as self-evident, and the practice is ripe for rethinking. However, if the genealogical critique is meant to be part of the case for abolition—that is, to be an argument for a movement to end the use of prisons—it has limitations.

The genealogical critique holds that the contemporary practice of imprisonment is a "legacy" of slavery. Let's consider this the standard formulation. Alternative formulations include asserting that prisons "are a structural inheritance of slavery," "are an institutional descendant of slavery," "are a heritage of slavery," "have historical resonances with slavery," "have their roots in slavery," "exhibit traces of slavery," or "are a surviving vestige of slavery"—all formulations to be found in Davis's writings on prisons.[42]

Now this way of putting things—that existing imprisonment practices are a legacy of slavery—might suggest that slavery and imprisonment are not only both wrong but wrong for the same reason. This is an argumentative strategy that Marx often employed in his critique of capitalism. He would identify common features of slavery and serfdom (features that were then, and now, commonly held to be wrong) and then attempt to show that capitalism had these same features despite appearances to the contrary. All three systems, he maintained, are dehumanizing and despotic forms of involuntary servitude. Davis, too, can be plausibly read as claiming that imprisonment is, essentially, a form of slavery and should therefore be opposed on the same moral grounds. Yet this argument, already addressed, is not a genealogical critique, as its soundness does not depend on a historical connection between slavery and the prison. It depends only on both practices being wrong for the same or similar reasons.

"Legacy" could mean something like "remnant" or "outdated"—in effect, an obsolete holdover from another time, as when Davis speaks of the "vestiges" of slavery found in prisons.[43] The practice of imprisonment should have fully collapsed with the abolition of slavery, yet its ruins continue to impact our present. Here the general moral takeaway is that prisons had nefarious uses in the past (to facilitate and extend slavery, say), and they serve no useful purpose in the present, nor will they in the future. However, this would beg the question against reformers, who believe that incarceration has good and bad uses in the present and, with appropriate reforms, could be used solely for legitimate purposes in the future.

To have "roots" in slavery might suggest that slavery *nourishes*—that is, remains a causal ingredient in reproducing—current practices of imprisonment. Slavery, even long after it was abolished in the United States, has caused generations of people to be deeply disadvantaged. This unrectified disadvantage makes many vulnerable to incarceration. Prisons are full of people who were socioeconomically disadvantaged prior to their imprisonment.[44] The descendants of American slaves continue to be among the most disadvantaged groups in the United States, and also represent a strikingly disproportionate share of the prison population. If an explanatory cause of this overrepresentation among the imprisoned is the fact that the harms of slavery have not been fully rectified or compensated, then this clearly calls for redress.

Yet it is unclear why such rectification should take the form of prison abolition. The root of the problem is not the existence of prisons but pervasive and deeply unjust socioeconomic disadvantage more broadly. The appropriate response would therefore be to remove the disadvantages that make the descendants of slaves vulnerable to being arrested and imprisoned. This would mean not only ensuring due process and the rule of law but also preventing racial discrimination, securing equal educational opportunity for all, enhancing employment opportunities for the jobless and underemployed, securing housing for the homeless, protecting worker rights, increasing income subsidies for the poor, de-concentrating and redistributing wealth, guaranteeing universal health care, politically empowering the socially marginalized, and other such measures.

It could be argued that what has been "inherited" from the era of slavery are ideologies and institutions (racism and prisons) that *perform the same functions* in the present. In effect, these functions persist as inherent (or near inherent) features of prisons and related ideologies. This is a version of the "ineradicable logic" of institutions thesis, which I will address in the next chapter.

If "legacy" means something like "inherited from" or "handed down from the past," we still must ask whether the *objectionable* features were also bequeathed and if so, whether these can be removed without destroying the inherited item itself or turning it into something else entirely. A business that operated according to racist values in the past when in the hands of its previous owners might operate now in a way that satisfies requirements of racial justice because the business is under the direction of new, antiracist owners. Institutions are more like property than like genes. Those who "inherit" institutions have considerable control over what they will be like going forward, because they can adopt different aims, can change institutional rules and procedures, can alter the rights and responsibilities of those who participate in the institution, and can choose new personnel, including new leadership. Consider the many multigender and multiracial colleges and universities (like my home institution) that used to be open only to economically privileged, Protestant, gender-conforming white men.

This point is entirely consistent with—indeed, a necessary feature of—a broadly historical materialist outlook. Marx thought that the means of production in the hands of the bourgeoisie were instruments of subjugation and exploitation. But once the proletariat takes hold of them, placing them under worker control and no longer using them as private capital to maximize profit, these means—whose immense productive power has been cultivated under capitalism—will be the basis for freedom, community, and material prosperity for all. The fact that these highly developed means of production would be a legacy of "wage slavery" is not a good reason, according to Marx, to refuse to use them under socialism.

Marx made a similar argument about the state itself. He believed that under capitalism the modern bureaucratic state functions as the executive committee for arranging the affairs and advancing the interests of the bourgeoisie. Yet, after the revolution, the state would be an emancipatory instrument in the hands of the proletariat, who would use it to dismantle the oppressive elements of capitalism and lay the groundwork for communism.

Perhaps the penal arm of the state (like, say, intergenerational monetary bequests) is a feature of the old and decaying social order best discarded in the new. This is one way of interpreting the call for prison abolition—that when the truly free society is successfully built, it will be, and should be, one without prisons. This claim cannot be established, however, by merely pointing to the fact that prisons were forged within and have been inherited from an unjust social order. Capitalism, by Marx's own accounting, develops many things (including labor-saving technology and efficient ways of organizing work) that we can expect to be preserved in a socialist society.

Reform and Redress

Prisons as we know them, now and in the past, are often dehumanizing, horrid, even torture chambers. Many existing prisons have far too much in common with slavery.[45] Injustices in the wider social structure can also affect the fairness and legitimacy of penalizing crime through incarceration and prison labor.

Imprisoning members of oppressed groups for serious wrong-doing, though sometimes necessary to protect the vulnerable, is a morally troubling practice. These prisoners are due redress in the form of corrective justice. Had they received such redress, these prisoners may not have found themselves running afoul of the law. Forcing them to work while incarcerated, though not slavery, can be a substantial insult, particularly when they are the descendants of slaves. The state, whose very legitimacy depends on securing just conditions for all, lacks the moral standing to condemn much of the wrongdoing it penalizes, as it is often responsible, in part, for the circumstances that lead to crime. And it cannot justify requiring the unjustly disadvantaged to work to cover the costs of their imprisonment when it has so utterly failed to ensure justice in the society from which these prisoners come.

But punishing the justly convicted by forcing them to do unpaid work is not always unfair, let alone an instance of slavery. The situation might seem otherwise because of injustices that lie elsewhere, including within the broader criminal justice system. Often the underlying problem is that the prison sentence is unwarranted or unfair given the nature of the crime (for instance, needlessly harsh). Or, given structural injustices in the broader society, the state lacks the moral standing to punish the criminal offense (for example, when it penalizes economic crimes among the poor). Or prison conditions are already so needlessly severe that forced labor would be cruel and degrading. And, all too often, a prisoner did not commit the crime for which they were convicted, or, even if they did, due process standards were not adequately met and so they were not convicted fairly.

All this, I believe, the prison reformer can readily, even strongly, endorse. Indeed, for these reasons, some existing prisons and perhaps some whole prison systems should be closed. Yet these conclusions, as distressing and infuriating as they are, do not constitute a compelling case for abolishing the general practice of imprisonment. Prison, no matter how humane or well administered, is an undesirable place to be. There can be no doubt about that. This of course is part of the point, at least insofar as the incarceration is a form of punishment. So far, what the abolitionist case against prisons suggests is the urgent need, not only for prison reform, but for broader social-structural reform. In this way at least, abolitionists and radical reformers are often, despite appearances, on the same side.

CHAPTER 3

A Broken System?
Racism and Functional Critique

The abolitionist case against the practice of imprisonment is complex. As discussed in the previous chapter, there is the charge that prisons are dehumanizing and related to slavery in ways which make their continued existence objectionable. But another criticism comes up repeatedly in abolitionist writings, one that centers on the function of prisons.

The functional argument takes multiple forms, which can be classified into four general versions: that the function of the prison is economic exploitation (or the facilitation of such exploitation); that the function of the prison is racial subjugation (or to perpetuate racism); that the function of the prison is to repress political resistance; and that the function of the prison is to conceal intractable social problems. These claims are best understood as conclusions of a type of social analysis, familiar from some varieties of Marxism and critical theory, that I call *functional critique*.

I want to briefly elaborate on each of these claims and offer a more precise formulation of the structure of functional critique. But my principal focus here is the claim that prisons serve a racist function. (The other three claims get more extensive treatment elsewhere in the book.) Focusing on the case of racism illustrates the power of this form of social critique but also highlights its limits. The functional critique of prisons, I will argue, does not show that prisons should be abolished rather than reformed. But, understood in a way I'll explain, the critique can establish that, in the United States at least, we should radically reduce our reliance on prisons.

As a reminder, by "the prison" I don't mean merely the facilities in which prisoners are confined. Nor do I have in mind particular prisons, like Soledad, San Quentin, or Rikers. I mean the general institutionalized *practice* of incarceration, which forcibly confines prisoners within an enclosed space, physically separates them from the public, claims custodial guardianship over them, subjects them to the directives of prison officials, and treats them in these ways as a penalty for criminal offenses. The prison is an institutional apparatus of captivity, surveillance, and social control, an institution that cannot operate without coercion and severe constraints on prisoners' freedom.

Davis on the Functions of Prisons

The form of functional critique that Angela Davis favors draws heavily on Marxism. She believes that capitalism (like slavery and serfdom) is a degrading and despotic system of involuntary servitude. The function of capitalism, she maintains, is not to meet human needs through the efficient production and free exchange of useful commodities but to maximize profit for the benefit of a small ruling elite. These financial gains are garnered at the expense of those outside the ruling class (primarily wage laborers) and are not the product of "free" exchange but extracted through force, theft, and fraud. This wrongful extraction of profit takes many forms. There are, for instance, institutions that ostensibly serve the public good but, in fact, serve only (or mainly) to maximize corporate profit. Davis believes this is true of prison systems (see Chapter 4).[1]

Davis is not a class reductionist or an orthodox Marxist. She does not believe that all oppression is ultimately or primarily a form of economic exploitation or class-based subjugation. She maintains, like others in the black radical tradition, that *racism* is also a form of oppression. Although often intimately related to economic subordination, racism is a distinct injustice, wrongful in itself. Davis holds that the practice of punitive incarceration is racist, perpetuates racism, and creates new modes of racism.[2]

According to Davis, the prison also serves as an instrument for political repression (see Chapter 1).[3] It should not be surprising that those subject to economic exploitation and racial domination often resent and resist the people and institutions that oppress them. Despite the risks involved, some will naturally refuse to submit to subordination and servitude. When people do rise up to oppose an unjust social system—whether individually or collectively, spontaneously or in a coordinated fashion—the state uses the penal system to put down or contain this resistance and to deter others from engaging in similar defiance.

Prison, Davis argues, "serves as a place to warehouse people who represent major social problems."[4] Capitalist predation creates and exacerbates social problems—poverty, homelessness, violence, disorder, mental illness, and drug abuse. These problems cannot be solved within the existing social framework. Those who cannot be integrated into the current market economy in a way that is consistent with maximizing corporate profit are often incarcerated to keep them from public view. This circumstance obscures deep dysfunction in the social system or presents it as an "ordinary" problem of crime.

I turn now to the point and structure of functional critique. Not all function *statements* ("the function of X is Y") are offered as explanatory or critical. Sometimes the ascription of a function to an institution is simply a matter of identifying one of its purported beneficial consequences, suggesting an answer to the question, "What good does X do?" Or one might be identifying the institution's official purpose, that is, the justifying aim generally offered for why the institution is worthwhile and should continue to exist.

Davis isn't doing either of these. She is not talking about the penal system's "beneficial" consequences but its more destructive ones. The fact that some group (for example, capitalists or the ruling class) benefits from imprisonment is, for Davis, part of what makes prisons objectionable. She doesn't think prisons serve to prevent crime, to rehabilitate offenders, or to impose the suffering that offenders "deserve." For her, to identify the "real" function of the prison is to explain why the prison continues to exist despite not actually serving its official purpose, and, on this basis, to morally condemn it.

The explanatory and the critical dimensions of functional critique are closely related but can be examined separately. So we could set aside whether the consequence is good or bad and focus on whether identifying the consequence really explains what it purports to explain. And we could leave aside the explanatory question and attend to whether the consequence is as bad as the critique implies. However, to arrive at abolitionist conclusions using functional analysis, the explanatory claim must *ground* the critical claim. That is to say, prisons must persist *because* they serve an oppressive function. As I will attempt to make clear, it is not enough to show (assuming it can be shown) that prisons came into existence to serve these functions. Nor is it sufficient to show that prisons take the horrid form they typically do because they serve oppressive functions. If prisons can be reformed so that they are humane, fair to prisoners, and only perform legitimate functions, then functional critique cannot yield abolitionist conclusions. (Prison abolition might, however, be justified on some other grounds.)

In critically examining functional critiques of prisons, I am not challenging the validity of functional explanation as such.[5] Nor do I say that functional explanations of social phenomena are never sound. Instead, I want to offer an interpretation of Davis's functional claims about prisons and ask whether, if true, these claims would justify the abolition of prisons.

The General Form of Functional Critique

Radical functional critiques can sometimes seem compelling because they are offered in vague, esoteric, or metaphorical language. One often hears social criticism that takes the form, "The system isn't broken; it's operating the way it's supposed to."[6] Or some will say, "These oppressive consequences are to be expected, given the *logic* of the system." Such familiar functionalist claims suggest that "the system" cannot be reformed or fixed, only done away with or replaced with something entirely different. However, to fully assess the power of such functional critiques, greater precision is needed.

To say "the (or a) function of X is Y," where this is meant as a critique of X, the critical theorist is essentially making three related claims:

I. X causes (or is a causal contributor to) Y (in social system S).
II. The fact that X causes Y explains X (or some important feature of X).
III. Y is unjust or oppressive (or facilitates an oppressive S).

The target of a functional critique can be an institution, a belief system, or both simultaneously. Let's say X is an institution (for example, a school or educational system). We can think of institutions as constituted by *a set of public rules, social roles, and goals*. This system of rules and roles enables and regulates sustained cooperation for some explicit purpose. (Schools have a schedule, a curriculum, and standards of evaluation; they have administrators, teachers, and students; and they aim to have students learn through formal instruction and examinations.) These rules specify procedures, lines of authority, prohibitions, prerogatives, and standards. Participants in the practice generally understand these rules and their institutional roles, but might not fully comply with the rules or carry out their role obligations conscientiously.

We can call the *goal* that core participants publicly avow the institution's *official purpose*. (And an institution can have more than one official purpose. So, for instance, a school might aim to prepare students for college, to teach them skills valued by the labor market, and to prepare them for responsible citizenship.) The institution may or may not achieve its official purpose (at least not fully). Officials may, and often do, revise rules and re-define roles or create new rules and roles so that the institution better achieves its aims or so that it continues to achieve its aims despite a changing environment.

Now, the participants in an institution (or some powerful subset) may privately share an aim that diverges from or even conflicts with the institution's official purpose. (Perhaps school administrators or teachers surreptitiously seek to indoctrinate students into a particular political ideology or to inculcate a dis-position to always submit to authority.) Let's call this concealed or unacknowledged aim a *covert purpose*. The *operative aim(s)* of participants in an institution—that is, the goal(s) they *actually* attempt to achieve—can be an official purpose, a covert pur-pose, or both.

Following Robert Merton, I call something a function of X only if it is an *actual effect* of X.[7] When an observable causal con-sequence of an institution is generally aligned with the official purpose of that institution, we can refer to this effect as the insti-tution's *manifest function*. (The students learn in accordance with the school's official curriculum.) The institution is functioning as it purports to (though not necessarily as well as it could). An institu-tion can be malformed or broken such that it fails to perform its official purpose or such that it performs the purpose poorly. Here we say that the institution is *malfunctioning* or *dysfunctional*.

A causal consequence of an institution that helps to explain the institution but is not the institution's official purpose is a *latent* function of the institution. (The students who attended the school accept a partisan ideology or are submissive in the face of authoritarian demands.) This latent function may be attributable to the covert purposes of the institution's participants (or some powerful subset thereof). Here, a concealed, unacknowledged, or maybe even disavowed goal is the real operative aim, notwithstanding any official purposes the institution is said to serve.

However, the function—that is, the consequences—may be unintended or unrecognized by participants in the institution. Or—and this point is underappreciated—even if *some* participants do seek these consequences, they may lack the collective efficacy to bring them about. (So, for example, teachers may try to indoctrinate their students but fail miserably; yet the students, because of some unnoticed structural feature of the school, come to accept the political ideology nonetheless.) The welcome consequences are, with respect to these participants' conscious agency, merely fortuitous. Yet to be the *function* of the institution, these consequences cannot be mere happenstance. They must, in some way, explain the institution itself. I'll return in a moment to how an institution's unintended consequences could have this kind of explanatory significance.

But first, what facts about an institution is a functional critique meant to explain? Since the causal consequences of an existing institution are the relevant explanatory facts, functional critiques are not generally invoked to explain why an institution came to exist to begin with. A functional analysis may, however, explain why the institution *persists* despite changes elsewhere in the society. Or it may help us understand why the institution is so *resilient* in the face of robust attempts to do away with it.

The function of an institution might explain its *structure*—its specific rules and its social roles. Or, finally, it might explain why the institution operates the way it does—why its participants take the individual and collective actions that they do.

One explanatory value of the manifest/latent distinction is to make sense of an institution that doesn't appear to achieve its official purpose. Davis does this when she suggests that prison systems persist (indeed have even expanded) despite the fact that prisons don't actually prevent crime (their ostensible aim). She then argues that their covert purpose or unintended or unrecognized consequence is something else—economic exploitation, racial domination, political repression, and the disguising of social problems. In other words, the *latent* function of prisons is creating or maintaining various forms of oppression.

Now let's suppose the target of functional critique is a widely held belief system. (Think of the system of belief that some call "neoliberalism.") These beliefs may not be fully conscious and might be merely implicit in the dispositions and utterances of those who share them. (Maybe the faith that competitive markets always promote human welfare despite the inequality they generate is merely assumed rather than a considered judgment.) There can also be shifts over time in the content of the belief system without the system losing its basic integrity. (Neoliberalism can concede that some government regulation benefits the public and that not all public functions should be privatized.) When such a belief system shapes identities, encourages habits, or otherwise influences action, it can have significant social effects. Many who are unfamiliar with or openly reject the belief system can nonetheless be greatly impacted (for good or ill) by the fact that *others* embrace and act on these beliefs.

Sometimes the beliefs in question have been intentionally propagated to effect certain social consequences. When demagogues or propagandists are successful, we can say that the function of these ideas is to bring about these actors' conscious (though perhaps covert) purposes. At other times, the beliefs are developed and spread more spontaneously. Either no one (or almost no one) seeks to give them the social impact they have; or, though some seek this outcome, they lack the capacity to bring it about. Yet the wide acceptance of the belief system is explained by its social consequences.

A functional critique of a belief system is based, in part, on the bad practical consequences wide acceptance of the beliefs are said to have for society or some social group. These consequences generally include fostering or reinforcing an unjust social arrangement. However, despite these unwelcome social consequences, it would be irrational to reject the belief system and wrong to encourage others to reject it if the beliefs in question are true, morally sound, or otherwise epistemically well grounded. Consider the belief that the overwhelming power of the state would quickly crush any violent rebellion. Provided the belief is true, it should not be rejected, though its spread could lead to passivity or resignation in the face of political repression. The spirit of resistance should not be advanced with false or misleading claims. To avoid tacitly endorsing the use of propaganda, functional critique typically includes attributing some distortion, moral error, or misrepresentation to the belief system in question. Indeed, on some accounts, the oppressive social consequences are brought about through the cognitive or moral failings of the belief system. (Ordinary working people suffer, it might be thought, because of the wide acceptance of the false belief that high economic inequality, concentrated wealth, and low taxes are to everyone's advantage.)

These *social illusions* lead people to fail to recognize or fully appreciate that they are situated within (and might be unwittingly perpetuating) oppressive social relations. This misperception of reality or faulty moral reasoning affects the subjects' cognitive, emotional, and volitional relations to the social world they inhabit and, consequently, influences their conduct and structures their social practices. Belief systems that play this distinctive role in society are, in Marxist parlance, *ideologies*.

Racism and Prisons

Davis has long held that antiracism should play a central role in abolitionist theory and practice.[8] She argues, "If we are already persuaded that racism should not be allowed to define the planet's future and if we can successfully argue that prisons are racist institutions, this may lead us to take seriously the prospect of declaring prisons obsolete."[9]

Notice the form of argument. Racism (like slavery) is a grave wrong and widely known to be so. The practice of imprisonment, despite appearances to the contrary, is a form of racism. Given the principle "If X is a grave wrong, then X should be stopped," we can conclude that the practice of imprisonment should be ended. Accordingly, Davis holds that antiracist activism should include advocating for the abolition of prisons (and some activists in the Black Lives Matter movement have taken up the call.[10]). The key burden of this argument is to show that (and perhaps how) prisons are inherently or incorrigibly racist.

In calling prisons "racist," Davis is making a number of distinct but related claims about the relationship between racism and imprisonment. She says, for example, "Law-and-order discourse is racist, the existing system of punishment has been deeply defined by historical racism. Police, courts, and prisons are dramatic examples of institutional racism."[11] The first and third of these claims are, I believe, properly understood as conclusions of functional critique.

The claim about law-and-order rhetoric centers on the role of *ideologies* in unjust societies. For instance, racist belief systems can serve to legitimize incarcerating masses of people. Widespread racial prejudice, which often underlies or exacerbates fear of crime, leads people to take aggressive and sometimes drastic measures to protect themselves from perceived threats to their liberty, person, or property. Davis argues that the idea that there is a "black crime problem" is an ideological distortion with deep roots in slavery and convict leasing and is now fostered by mass media depictions of black life.[12] Ideological racism represents black persons as disposed to criminality, which in turn seems to license violent tactics by law enforcement and even by private citizens (such as George Zimmerman killing Trayvon Martin in Florida in 2012 or Gregory and Travis McMichael killing Ahmaud Arbery in Georgia in 2020).

Moreover, there are belief systems that, ostensibly, are not about race at all yet nonetheless serve to legitimate the subordination of racially stigmatized groups. "Law-and-order," "tough on crime," and "war on drugs" rhetoric is often said to function as ideological legitimation for white supremacy. What appears to be a race-neutral justification for aggressive law enforcement to "fight crime" or to ensure "public safety" serves as a rationalization for race-based domination, humiliation, brutality, and cruelty.

Now if the *sole* reason that imprisonment is accepted as legitimate is due to racism or some other ideology, then a functional critique would go a long way toward establishing the need for prisons to be abolished. If, however, there is a plausible public justification for the practice—say, that it is a fair and effective way to control serious crimes—then the justification must be shown to fail if the functional critique is to justify abolition. The existence of a bad justification for a practice, even if widely accepted, does not preclude there being a good one. And the fact that some act on a bad justification doesn't mean that none act, or could be brought to act, on a good one.

When Davis asserts that prisons are an instance of institutional racism, she is not suggesting that their *manifest* function is racial domination. Officials of the U.S. criminal justice system do not proclaim publicly that a goal of law enforcement is, say, to maintain white supremacy. Rather, Davis believes that racial domination is a *latent* function of contemporary prisons.

Whatever its manifest function, an institution's goals are racist when the covert aims of its officials (particularly those with the power to make and revise the institution's rules) are to oppress or otherwise harm members of a racial group. The institution's rules may be race-neutral in their explicit content yet be designed to bring about or maintain the subjugation of a racially stigmatized group. It would be appropriate to strongly condemn such an institution even if its constitutive rules fail to secure its reprehensible goals. Ineffectiveness does not insulate an institution from moral criticism. But it would not be correct to attribute a latent *function* to the institution unless its covert purposes are actually achieved.

Even if an institution's officials don't have racist goals, the institution would still be racist if its rules, however subtly, are racially biased or discriminatory. These rules might have been fashioned, perhaps in the distant past, with racist intent but are now applied without awareness of their origins. Or the rules, despite not having been designed with this end in view, may nonetheless unfairly advantage one racial group over another without officials noticing the inequity. Racism might be present in how rules are applied and also in whether rules are complied with. The institution's goals and rules could be legitimate, but administrators may fail to impartially apply and consistently comply with these rules due to their (perhaps unconscious) racial prejudice. No matter the manifest function of the institution, when this distorting racist influence is pervasive yet goes uncorrected by officials, we are dealing with a case of institutional racism.

This framework, which I call *intrinsic* institutional racism, captures much of what Davis says when she insists that prisons are a case of institutional racism. For instance, she claims, "There are persisting structures of racism, economic and political structures that *do not openly display their discriminatory strategies*, but nonetheless serve to keep communities of color in a state of inferiority and oppression" (emphasis added).[13] She also says, "When we consider the disproportionate number of people of color among those who are arrested and imprisoned, and the ideological role that imprisonment plays in our lives, I want to suggest that the prison population in [the United States] provides visible evidence of who is not allowed to participate in this democracy."[14]

Given long-standing stereotypes about so-called black criminality, prisons are an especially fertile site for the reproduction of racist ideology and the operation of institutional racism.[15] Indeed, Davis has suggested that because of the workings of the racialized prison system in the United States since the fall of formal slavery, blackness and criminality have come to be effectively equated, stigmatizing all black people (but especially young black men) and making them vulnerable to police abuse and incarceration regardless of whether they are actually guilty of any wrongdoing.[16] One might conclude then, on antiracist grounds, that prisons should be abolished rather than reformed.

This line of argument has much truth in it. Yet its implications for the reform-versus-abolition debate are unclear. On one reading, Davis is claiming that the ideological link between black (male) identity and criminality can be broken only by abolishing the prison system itself (at least within the United States). If no one goes to prison, then no one, including black people, can be regarded as a "criminal." But this can't be right. One could be thought to be a criminal even if one never goes to prison or is never even arrested, as was true of most victims of lynching and as the tragic recent examples of Trayvon Martin and Ahmaud Arbery show. The racist stereotype is that black people are *disposed* to commit crimes, which does not depend on their being caught, charged, or caged. If the link between blackness and criminality is as strong as Davis suggests, then ending imprisonment for crimes won't be sufficient to break the link. For black people to be fully free of this form of racism, not only would the criminal justice system have to be abolished altogether but the very idea of "crime"—that is, serious law breaking—would have to be delegitimized or made obsolete as well.

There is no doubt that racially disparate imprisonment rates *reinforce* the ideological construct of the "black criminal" and nourish the irrational fear of black people. We should keep in mind, though, that racism operates in several institutional contexts, not just in the criminal justice system. And stereotypes about black people being stupid and lazy have existed as long as (if not longer than) stereotypes about black people being violent and criminal.[17] Schools, for example, are pervaded by stereotypes about black people's cognitive deficiencies, and there is a stubborn racially marked academic achievement gap.[18] Yet despite these lamentable facts, we would not call to abolish schools, only to improve them and make them more equitable. Nor do we call for the abolition of jobs or workplaces because of the stereotype about black people being indolent or the long-standing racial disparities in employment that might seem to lend credence to the stereotype. Nor would we seek to abolish the institution of the family on the grounds that there are stigmatizing stereotypes about black reproductive and parental irresponsibility and that black families are disproportionately fragile and broken.

What this suggests is that charges of ideological and institutional racism can yield abolitionist conclusions only if the institution in question either is already irredeemably unjust (that is, apart from being racist) or performs no socially necessary function. These reflections on other kinds of institutions also suggest that, at least sometimes, we should devise ways to block or limit the influence of racial ideology and discriminatory practices within an institution rather than giving up altogether on the institution itself.

Ideological and institutional racism are powerful forces in prison systems in the United States and elsewhere. Yet there are many who are capable of sincerely rejecting racist beliefs and refraining from acting on racial biases. Racially prejudiced personnel—from the top of an organization down to the bottom ranks—can be identified and replaced. Racially discriminatory rules can be discovered, exposed, and discarded. Thus, uncovering the racism within existing prison systems, even when such racism has a long history or is pervasive, is not sufficient to establish that prisons should be abolished rather than reformed.

Whether we should be reformers or abolitionists will depend on at least the following: (1) whether imprisonment has a legitimate goal that would justify its inherent costs and risks; (2) whether criminal justice rules can be devised to fairly and effectively achieve this goal; (3) whether sufficient personnel can be recruited, trained, and relied upon to impartially and consistently follow these rules; and (4) whether there is a practically achievable alternative set of practices that could secure the same goal but with fewer harmful or costly consequences.

On the first question, I have already suggested that the answer is "yes" by arguing (in the previous chapter) that preventing great and irreparable harm is a legitimate aim of imprisonment. When the crimes are serious and those who commit them are culpable, a carceral penalty, if proportionate to the crime, is hard but not unfair treatment. This offers a partial answer to the second question about fair and effective rules, an answer I will develop further in chapters to come, along with an answer to the fourth question about non-carceral alternatives. The third question is difficult to answer in anything like a definitive way.

The personnel problem is particularly acute in deeply unjust societies like the United States, as I will discuss later in this chapter and in the next.

Functional Explanation and Unjust Social Systems

So far, I have discussed some ways that the consequences of imprisonment can be oppressive. I have also considered how latent functions of prisons can be oppressive when these functions depend on either covert goals or discriminatory institutional practices. Yet the truly radical dimensions of Davis's functional critique cannot be fully captured in these terms. For Davis, the racial disparity in imprisonment and the racialization of prisoners are not "incidental" features of capitalist society (say, the result of law-enforcement officials' correctable racial prejudice) but a *necessary* consequence of a capitalist system with roots in race-based slavery and colonialism.[19] To see the full implications of this idea, we must rely on a richer, but also a more controversial, conception of functional explanation.

The U.S. prison system is a vast network of carceral institutions, which includes federal and state prisons, municipal and county jails, and juvenile and immigrant detention centers. This network can operate only in conjunction with other institutions—primarily legislative bodies, law-enforcement agencies, courts, and parole or probation agencies. There is great variation in incarceration rates and penal policy across states and regions of the country. This complex system of institutions is not one superagent with cohesive plans and aims. It does not, nor can it, act with one mind.[20] Within any given sub-system, there will be officials and participants with conflicting goals and motives. Politicians, police officers, prosecutors, defense attorneys, judges, jurors, parole officers, prison administrators, and correctional officers often have divergent interests and ambitions. And they carry out their duties (whether conscientiously or poorly) in interaction not only with each other but also with persons suspected of crimes, persons accused of crimes, victims of crimes, witnesses, prisoners, and the formerly incarcerated. There is good reason to doubt that these diverse officials strategically coordinate their actions (or that they *could* coordinate their actions) to defend the interests of the ruling classes or white people. So, a functional critique of the U.S. prison system in terms of criminal justice officials' conscious but covert aims will be of limited value.

It might be more promising to attribute a *master function* to prisons: namely, that prisons serve to stabilize unjust social systems. The other functions attributed to prisons—racial domination, economic exploitation, political repression, obscuring social problems—are subsidiary or are to be understood in relation to this master function. Prisons perform this stabilizing function through, say, fostering racial division, incapacitating the most rebellious elements in society, deterring people from developing a revolutionary posture, protecting property claims from militant challenge, and so on.

The basic social-theoretic premise is that unjust modern societies are, by their nature, *unstable*. Thus, those that persist over time tend to develop and maintain prisons, which enable the survival of these oppressive social systems despite their inherent instability. To be sure, unjust social orders are not stabilized by penal regimes alone. Brute force is never sufficient. Ideologies also function to secure hierarchical and inegalitarian social systems. They do so by encouraging people not to question the system's legitimacy and by inducing the oppressed to believe that their obedience to law is not only prudent but morally required.

I think this framework fits much of what Davis says about the relation between prisons and unjust societies. For instance, she argues that the penal system functions as a weapon to preserve the status quo when resistance movements emerge to challenge the legitimacy of the social order.[21] She also argues that the "overriding" function of the prison is not crime control but social control and political containment—the repression of "proclivities" to challenge legal regulations and the extraction of total obedience to the law, particularly property laws, which protect the assets of the ruling class.[22]

Now the mere fact that prisons are functional for unjust societies doesn't show that prisons exist because (let alone only because) they are functional for unjust societies. (Pencils are functional for scratching that part of our back that is hard to reach, but that's not why pencils exist or continue to be produced.) The beneficial consequences for a ruling class could be a mere accident, an unintended byproduct of a practice that exists for other purposes. So what more has to be established for the master-function claim to be truly explanatory?

One way of making good on a functional explanation is to identify a *feedback loop*, say, from an ideology or institution to a pattern of causal consequences and from these consequences back to the ideology or institution itself. The ideology or institution persists *because* it has consequences that reinforce or preserve it. In other words, the persistence of the ideology or the institution (or the persistence of both) is explained (at least in part) *by* the ideology's or institution's functional consequences.

Along these lines, Davis identifies a process she calls a "self-reproducing cycle."[23] The prison, though not a belief system, can perform essentially the same function that ideologies do. An institution or social practice can serve an ideological function in that it can mislead us about or conceal important social facts. It can encourage or reinforce false beliefs about social reality, a misperception that can buttress an unjust status quo. In a society where racial ideology has currency, racially biased law-enforcement practices obscure the oppressive workings of capitalism. Capitalism creates joblessness, poverty, and desperation, which gives the oppressed an economic incentive to turn to the underground economy—the drug trade, prostitution, theft, robbery, illegal gambling, trafficking in stolen goods, and so on—and thus puts them at high risk for imprisonment. The long-standing and powerful stereotypes about black people as lazy and violent lead people to explain racial disparities in employment and imprisonment in terms of black people's moral failings, and the disparities themselves seem to "confirm" the stereotypes. Fear of the "black criminal" can appear to warrant strong retributive sentiments and to license practices of containment.[24] In this way, an ideology (racism) and an institution (the prison) can have social consequences that explain why the ideology and the institution persist.

The Limits of Functional Critique

Let's suppose prisons serve all the functions Davis attributes to them, including the master function of stabilizing unjust social orders. Still, I don't think we can conclude from this that we should end the practice of imprisonment. Why not? Well, we'd first have to see whether prisons also serve any legitimate and vital functions. If they do and there is no functional equivalent within reach, we may need to reform the prison (or other related features of the society) so that prisons have fewer of the pernicious consequences Davis identifies. Or we may, if feasible, effect social changes that eventually eliminate the *need* for prisons. (For example, if there is very little serious crime, then drastic law-enforcement efforts aren't necessary.) Put more tersely, abolition would follow from this functional critique alone only if either there is a viable functionally equivalent institution or set of practices with fewer bad consequences, or there is no legitimate function that prisons serve.

Recall that prisons, like many other institutions, are capable of performing more than one function, even under the same social conditions. In fact, functional critique does not rule out an institution serving both a latent function and its manifest function. Indeed, an institution could serve its oppressive functions *better* if it also achieves, to some extent, its official purpose. In that way, the institution's unjust structure wouldn't be readily apparent and so would be less likely to engender militant resistance. (Capitalism, for example, does produce many desirable consumer goods and services and enables some members of the working class to become wealthy.)

So the fact that imprisonment serves a racist, repressive, or exploitative function is compatible with it also serving to protect people from unjust aggression against their liberty, person, or possessions. Of course, the prison cannot serve these oppressive functions and still be *just*, even if it does manage to prevent some serious crime. And this is one reason why radical reform efforts, within the criminal justice system and elsewhere, are so urgently needed.

The abolitionist could concede that prisons serve multiple functions yet insist that we cannot have the legitimate manifest function of the prison (securing public safety) without its oppressive latent functions. What reason might we have to think this? Sometimes proponents of functional critique regard institutions (or at least some of them) as having an "ineradicable logic" or "essence" that is present whenever and wherever the institution in question exists. Let's consider this possibility with respect to prisons.

There's a weak sense in which an institution could have an essence: namely, its official purpose is one of its constitutive features. Incarceration is "imprisonment," strictly speaking, only if it is imposed as a crime-control measure. Otherwise the practice is something else, say, kidnapping or revenge. However, if the idea is that latent functions of an institution always remain intact regardless of changes in the institution's rules, procedures, social roles, or personnel and regardless of alterations in the surrounding social context, then the notion is not very plausible.

It is undeniable that an institution could have one set of consequences in circumstances C_1 but an entirely different, even incompatible, set of consequences in circumstances C_2. Imagine, for instance, that C_1 is marked by severe racial and economic inequality but C_2 is not. An institution could be functional for more than one type of system, including just and unjust social systems. Schools—depending on what, whom, and how they teach and who does the teaching—are presumably functional both for capitalism and for socialism, for a highly unequal society and for an egalitarian one. A similar thing can be said about families and workplaces. So, as far as I can tell, we can't decide whether abolition is preferable to reform if all we know is that the relevant institution is functional for an oppressive system. Something more must be established.

Sticking with the idea that prisons have a master function, Davis could argue that racist, capitalist societies are actually *homeostatic systems*: their characteristic injustices endure because changes in one part of the system are adjusted for elsewhere such that oppression is maintained. Similar to the way that the human body adjusts to maintain body temperature and blood pressure, there are mechanisms that keep some groups stigmatized, exploited, and subordinated despite even dramatic shifts in the institutions of the society. The prison (like banishment, execution, and public torture in previous eras) might be thought to be one of these key mechanisms. Some unjust societies, on this account, are not just self-reproducing systems but *self-adjusting* systems.

The homeostatic thesis is a radical claim, one that is difficult to prove and may even be unfalsifiable. I'm not certain that Davis would endorse it. But some who emphasize the continuity between slavery, Jim Crow, and mass incarceration seem attracted to it. So, for the sake of argument, let's suppose the homeostatic thesis is true. What implications would it have for the reform-versus-abolition debate? I can think of two.

First, if an unjust society is really a homeostatic system, meaningful social change from *within* the system—that is, using socially accepted methods for bringing about social change—looks hopeless. Prison abolition, as a practical political aim, would likely have to be achieved using means that are widely condemned in the society. Homeostatic systems are composed of many interdependent and shifting parts and, despite their dynamism, have a tendency toward a relatively stable equilibrium. So if the basic elements of the social system remain intact, we have no reason to believe that the abolition of prisons would stop a functional equivalent from emerging or prevent an adjustment elsewhere in the system that brings it back to the status quo.

Second, suppose the prison is not just one of many elements in the social system but a *linchpin*—a key piece that holds the system together. It is, let us say, equivalent to a vital organ in the human body. In that case, anti-prison theory is most at home in a revolutionary political framework, and the point of anti-prison practice would be to destabilize the social system as a whole. On this way of thinking, the prison stands in the way of meaningful social change and must be brought down or made inoperative if structural transformation is to occur. Indeed, some black radicals regard prisoners (or some subset of them) as indispensable members of the revolutionary force who, as political prisoners, must be liberated if the emancipatory effort is to succeed (see Chapter 1).

However, this political vision shifts the focus away from the prison as such to a debate over whether the society as a whole can be reformed or must be dismantled (perhaps forcibly) and reconstituted on a fundamentally different basis. This is undeniably a question worth asking, one that raises the theoretical and practical stakes considerably. But, on such a vision, prison abolition is essentially *tactical* and must then be assessed on grounds of practicality and likelihood of success versus alternative tactics. My primary concern in this book is with the radical political philosophy that treats a prison-free society and world, not as merely a strategic political aim, but as a fundamental moral objective.

A Moratorium on Imprisonment?

Let's set aside the homeostatic model of functional critique and its associated revolutionary tactics. Davis could still argue that prisons have a strong *tendency* or *propensity* to be used for bad ends, at least within certain social environments. Just as salt has the dispositional property to dissolve in water, prisons are disposed to contribute to oppression. On this account, prison reformers are like those who say, "Guns don't kill people; people kill people." Reformers contend that prisons can be used for good or bad purposes, depending on who governs them and whether they are used responsibly. This contention on the part of reformers, we must concede, is a half-truth.

Consider the current social environment in many wealthy capitalist societies, including the United States. Here, Davis would argue, we find political power and wealth concentrated in the hands of a small elite who benefit at the expense of the great majority. Poverty is deep and engenders despair, resentment, and shame. Many are frustrated and angry about their lack of economic security and limited access to quality education. Racial and other visible minorities are feared, despised, maligned, and routinely scapegoated. The general ethos is one of unbridled ambition, ruthless competition, and indifference to the suffering of the most vulnerable. Unsurprisingly, depression and drug abuse are widespread. So is interpersonal violence and fraud.

In such an environment, prisons, like guns, are a menace. The people who would wield them (or, anyway, far too many of them) are likely to do so irresponsibly or even maliciously. It is not that prisons are *inherently* dangerous or prone to abuse no matter the social environment. The social context matters enormously. In a racially stratified capitalist regime with immense socioeconomic inequality, low wages for the moderately skilled, and meager welfare entitlements for the poor and unemployed, we should *expect* incarceration to be widely abused and overused. The latent functions of imprisonment in the current unjust environment are, indeed, exploitation, political repression, and racial subjugation. Until we dramatically alter the social environment within which prisons operate, we should, it could be argued, put a *moratorium* on the use of prisons.

Such a moratorium is not tantamount to abolition, because it would not rule out prisons for all time and in all places. Prisons could still be legitimate under certain circumstance or in some locales, particularly when the social order is just or nearly so. It would, however, entail regarding their current use in places like the United States as illegitimate and intolerable. This moratorium would be based on the injustice of background structural conditions, not on a condemnation of existing prison conditions. That is, it should be distinguished from a moratorium based on the inhumane conditions inside specific prisons. Where prison conditions drop below human rights requirements, prisoners should be moved or released until the prison in question has been suitably reformed and renovated. The kind of moratorium I have in mind is also different from a moratorium on building new prison facilities, which some abolitionists advocate too.[25] Although I would be against expanding the prison system or increasing the prison population in the United States, I would not necessarily oppose building a new prison if it replaced one that was inhumane or unhabitable.

What I am discussing now is a moratorium on the practice of imprisonment that would be justified on grounds of systemic injustice. Were such a moratorium to be instituted in a particular society, the ban on imprisonment could be restricted to specific offenses or could include all offenses. The ban could also be limited to certain jurisdictions (where, say, social injustices are particularly egregious), or it could encompass the whole of U.S. society. At the most radical end of the spectrum, the moratorium would be society-wide and unrestricted as to offense. More limited moratoriums would be restricted to certain locales or to specific offenses (for example, less serious ones).

The call for a moratorium on the practice of imprisonment has serious merit. If the only legitimate purpose prisons served was rehabilitation, prison's great dangers and its burdens on the oppressed would probably be sufficient to justify even a radical moratorium. The tragic truth, though, is that in this same social environment and largely for the same reasons, the oppressed are vulnerable to violent aggression, not just from the police and correctional officers, but also at the hands of ordinary citizens, many of whom are oppressed themselves. It is the unjustly disadvantaged who are most vulnerable to being physically threatened, beaten, raped, or killed, sometimes by co-ethnics, neighbors, friends, intimate partners, and even family. As we attempt to transform our societies and world into something more just, we must take due care to protect the vital interests of the oppressed. We may invite greater dangers for them by removing the limited means of protection—police and prisons—that are available, as troubling and racist as they typically are.

This problem—how best to reduce the burdens on the oppressed—makes me hesitant to embrace a radical moratorium on the use of prisons. The proponent of a radical moratorium would hold that until we transform our society into something considerably more just, the state should admit no new persons to prison and should release those now incarcerated, regardless of the crimes for which these persons have been convicted and regardless of whether there is reason to think they committed these crimes. We must, they would insist, rely exclusively on non-carceral alternatives to control crime, even when dealing with the most serious crimes.

Rejecting a radical prison moratorium does put me (and some abolitionists) in the uncomfortable position of having to countenance that prison's benefits (crime prevention and prisoner rehabilitation) may be, at least temporarily, worth the prison system's oppressive costs, including its contribution to reinforcing racism. Still, we might defend a less radical prison moratorium. If instituted, it could mitigate ideological and institutional racism, thus making the toleration of punitive incarceration under unjust conditions a less bitter pill to swallow.

Suppose we reserved prison primarily for those who commit the most serious and egregious crimes. Here I have in mind primarily crimes against the person—murder, rape, kidnapping, child abuse, sex trafficking, and aggravated assault. We might also include arson, great financial crimes (think Bernie Madoff), and cybercrimes that threaten democracy. These acts cannot be justified or excused even under deeply unjust circumstances, and they typically cause lasting trauma or significant and irreparable harm. When feasible, these wrongs must be prevented to protect the vital interests of the vulnerable. Other offenses should either be decriminalized altogether or, where criminalization is warranted, carry lesser and non-carceral penalties (for example, fines, home confinement, restitution, temporary loss of privileges, community service, supervised probation, and electronic monitoring). Where incarceration is used, it should be joined with rehabilitative services, educational opportunities, job training, psychiatric and drug-abuse treatment, and preparation for reentry into society.

When considering a moratorium on prison use, it is best to distinguish what to do about potential future crime from what to do in response to crimes that have already happened. The limited moratorium position just described concerns preventing offenses yet to occur, either using prison (in limited cases) or non-carceral penalties. This is a call for radical sentencing reform and for a (temporary) halt to the use of punitive incarceration for minor and moderately serious crimes. An obvious corollary would be moderate *decarceration*. If a moratorium is warranted, then it would also make sense to release prisoners who have not committed the most serious crimes (for example, those whose worst offense is a drug-related crime). They could be treated as if they had fully served their time or, where necessary for public safety, alternative penalties could be imposed. And these newly released persons should be eligible for rehabilitative and reentry services.

Many prison reformers believe that the prison population in places like the United States should be dramatically reduced and that the prison system should not be expanded. They oppose mass incarceration and the structural injustices that led to it, but they are not opposed to incarceration as such. Rather than abolition, a restricted moratorium on the use of prisons could be the apt way to express their vision. So, although I am skeptical that the functional critique of prisons can justify abolitionist conclusions, it can, I think, help us see the urgency, not only for fundamental prison and sentencing reform, but also for broader structural reform of society itself.

Extrinsic Institutional Racism and Penal Policy

Davis's analysis of imprisonment as institutional racism offers wisdom and insight. Yet when cast as a functional critique, it cannot establish that the eradication of prisons is morally required or even desirable. That said, a *modified* form of this critique could help establish the need for a limited moratorium on prison use in the United States and elsewhere. It can do so without relying on controversial functional explanations and without insisting that there is always a covert racist purpose behind the practice of imprisonment.

Black radical thinkers developed the concept of *institutional racism* to account for the fact that racism can exert influence in institutional contexts where officials do not consciously hold or openly express racist beliefs and intentions.[26] Earlier I discussed *intrinsic* institutional racism, with a focus on covert goals and discriminatory practices. However, institutional racism can also be *extrinsic*. An institution's policies can be racist, not only in virtue of the racist attitudes or goals of those who make and implement policy, but also in virtue of the *consequences* of an institution's policies, even when these consequences are unintended or unforeseen.

Extrinsic institutional racism occurs when officials use a policy that is race-neutral in content and public justification but nevertheless has a significant or disproportionately negative impact on a disadvantaged racial group. Those who make and apply the policies need not intend this result and may not themselves harbor racist attitudes. The institution's practices are nonetheless wrong, because they perpetuate the negative effects of ongoing or past racist actions and because they thereby encourage racist attitudes and stereotypes.

Some social groups are already disadvantaged by racism, and an institution that is not intrinsically racist may still play a role in reinforcing the oppression of these groups. These detrimental effects can lead some to believe that the disadvantaged occupy their low social station because of their own moral failings or inherent inferiority, inviting the conclusion that they (rather than the social structure) should be blamed for any failure to flourish. The institution may not itself be responsible for the group's prior disadvantages, and the racism the institution is complicit with may be *extrinsic* to the institution itself. Nevertheless, *corrective justice*—the principles that govern how we should respond to and rectify injustice—may demand that the public actively seek to reverse or mitigate these oppressive institutional effects. This reduction or shift in the weight of oppression could be achieved through the implementation of policies that would have a less adverse effect on disadvantaged racial groups.

Davis thinks that the destructive power of the "black criminal" notion—an ideological idea—cannot be defused unless we abolish prisons. In the United States, black people are disproportionately locked up, and this might continue to be the case even if intrinsic institutional racism within the criminal justice system were eradicated. After all, joblessness, poverty, and educational disadvantage are strongly correlated with criminal offending, and black people are disproportionately unemployed, poor, and educationally disadvantaged. If part of the worry is that racial disparities in imprisonment seem to "confirm" stereotypes about black criminality, thereby reinforcing antiblack ideology, then eliminating or reducing these disparities would seem like a logical response. The question is whether the criminal justice system should play a role in this.

If, as Davis maintains, the practice of imprisonment further marginalizes racially stigmatized and disadvantaged social groups, this is a reason to change penal policy even if incarcerating black people who commit crimes is not inherently racist and prisons actually prevent crime. If we could secure a reasonable level of public safety without increasing the burdens on the oppressed or reinforcing negative racial stereotypes, then we should opt for these less harmful policies. In particular, if it could be shown that relying largely on non-carceral policies would adequately control crime but with less adverse impact on racially stigmatized groups, then a prison moratorium (whether radical or limited) might be justified or even morally required.

The basic idea is this. We should work to correct the structural injustices that engender crime *and* lighten the penalties on oppressed offenders where possible even if this would cost the public a lot more than simply relying on incarceration alone, and even if this would mean, at least in the short term, that we all must live with somewhat higher levels of crime.

CHAPTER 4

The Prison Industrial Complex: Profit, Privatization, and the Circumstances of Injustice

Some abolitionists call for the dismantling of the "prison industrial complex." This form of abolition is in many ways insightful and appealing, for reasons I will discuss. Yet as a critique of punitive incarceration it also has serious limitations. After laying out these insights and shortcomings, I want to offer a defense of the use of nonprofit prison privatization in limited contexts—that is, in societies that, while maintaining some degree of legitimacy, are marred by serious structural injustices.

Some otherwise sympathetic to the abolitionist cause stop short of calling for a complete ban on prisons. They allow that incarceration—whether as detention, rehabilitation, punishment, or incapacitation—has (or at least could have) a legitimate public function. Yet they are deeply troubled by the ways that privatization, commerce, and profit figure in many prison systems, particularly those in the United States. Thus, taking inspiration from Angela Davis, they call for an end to the prison industrial complex, though not necessarily to prisons as such. Those committed to a more radical abolitionist vision see the complete eradication of prisons as a long-term objective but sometimes treat the abolition of the prison industrial complex as an intermediate goal. Decoupling incarceration from capitalist enterprise is, for them, a necessary step toward a prison-free world.

One of Davis's core objections to incarceration is that, as generally practiced, it is an immoral fusion of ineffective state crime-control measures, the privatization of public functions, and the maximization of corporate profit. Davis seeks to abolish prisons partly because she views them as components of a vast and destructive "prison industrial complex."[1] This designation, she tells us, is meant to draw attention to the fact that prison construction, ownership, administration, and services, along with prison labor, attract large amounts of private capital, and that commercial profit from prisons is a driver of mass incarceration.

In using the expression "prison industrial complex," Davis is doing more than highlighting the commercial functions of carceral practices. She is making obvious connections with the "military industrial complex."[2] The moneymaking dimension is a big part of the moral indictment, as is the tendency of both complexes to rely on "security" as ideological justification. Prison systems and the military also use similar technology, and there are military prisons. But there are two further dimensions to Davis's critique. The first is the fact that prisons often function as machinery of war and as means of political repression, as discussed in Chapter 1. The second is the fact that the practice of imprisonment (which necessarily relies on police officers and prison guards) is an inherently violent enterprise. This was discussed in Chapter 2 when I considered justifications for preventative harm and set aside pacifism as a basis for prison abolition. So, the dimension of the prison industrial complex yet to be considered is the connection between incarceration and capitalist enterprise, or, as Davis sometimes puts it, the "business-government linkages" in the penal system.[3]

Incarceration as Detention

As discussed, incarceration has several purposes. I have mainly focused on incarceration when its purpose is punitive—that is, to penalize those convicted of crimes. To better grasp abolitionist objections to the prison industrial complex, the use of incarceration as pretrial detention (or what might be better called "pre-conviction detention") must be addressed.

Let's distinguish two pretrial periods. First, there is the period directly after arrest, when law-enforcement agents take a suspect (perhaps against their will) into custody for questioning or to face formal charges, but prior to formal charges being brought and prior to a formal plea on the part of the accused. The accused will be incarcerated during this period, which ideally should be brief (hours or days; not weeks or months, certainly not years). Second, there is the period directly after a formal plea of "not guilty" but prior to a trial to determine guilt. (This is "pretrial detention" strictly speaking.)

There are two plausible justifications for detention in jail. The first is that there are strong reasons to believe that the accused will not appear for trial or hearings or (what amounts to the same) will refuse to submit to accountability measures. The second is that there are strong reasons to believe that the accused is a serious danger to others and therefore incapacitation is warranted.

It is worth noting that to completely abolish incarceration as pretrial detention would mean that the public would have to rely on voluntary compliance with court orders and that the police would be prohibited from forcibly arresting suspects, even those accused of the most serious crimes and those known to be highly dangerous. If there are less harmful alternatives that would adequately ensure that the accused will submit to accountability measures (for instance, cash bail, supervised release, or electronic monitoring), then these would be preferable to incarceration. There may be some question about the costs of these alternatives (and who should pay them) that would make incarceration preferable and defensible. But I will largely leave this issue aside.

Now these non-carceral alternatives could lead to exploitation in commercial bail agreements and profit from electronic monitoring technology. There are opponents of the prison industrial complex who want to abolish commercial bail services and even cash bail itself. Under current circumstances, there is the worry that this could lead to more people in jail (and for longer) or to greater electronic monitoring and thus greater state surveillance, which some abolitionists, including Davis, also oppose. Some might argue, though, that if cash bail as a practice is permissible, prohibiting commercial bail would be an unfair interference with personal liberty. Why shouldn't the accused (or their family or friends) be permitted to make a contract with another private actor to share the cost and risk of bail?

If bail were always set at a cost the accused could be expected to pay relying solely on their own personal financial resources, commercial bail wouldn't be necessary. Bail might be reasonably set, though, on the assumption that friends or family will help with the costs. When such voluntary financial assistance is forthcoming, this not only suggests that the accused has strong ties to the community (and so is unlikely to flee the jurisdiction) but also that friends or family members are confident that the accused will appear for trial and hearings (or could be brought to do so through persuasion or informal pressure). If the default assumption is that friends and family will help, then it is not unreasonable (and perhaps wise) to sometimes set bail somewhat beyond the personal means of the accused.

Yet, the fact that a person lacks friends or family with the resources or requisite trust doesn't mean the person won't show up for trial. I'm inclined to think that such a person should probably be permitted to use commercial bail services, as this may be their only means to assure the court that they will make court appearances when called. A bail-bond agent would be unlikely to make such an agreement, though, if they lacked the power of arrest (or at least of electronic monitoring and collateral confiscation). Otherwise, commercial bail service companies would run an unreasonably high risk of default, perhaps making the enterprise unprofitable or very likely to fail. These companies are effectively assuring the court that they will ensure that the accused will appear in court. They are thereby exercising the equivalent of policing powers, despite being private organizations.

The advocate for the abolition of the prison industrial complex might insist that the public fully cover the costs of electronic monitoring, supervised release, and law enforcement to ensure that the accused appears in court. This would eliminate the need for bail altogether (though some among the accused may prefer bail to electronic monitoring) and therefore limit the financial burdens on the accused and their loved ones and reduce the extent to which criminal justice is a commercial enterprise. I find this position compelling.

Indeed, the abolitionist could go further. Where the criminal justice system is fair and widely believed to be so (which is not the case in the United States), we should expect citizens to appear for trial when the public (through its official representatives) has accused them of committing crimes. It should be mutually understood to be their civic responsibility and moral duty. Accordingly, it could be argued that since the accused has yet to be convicted, the presumption of innocence suggests that neither jail nor bail nor electronic monitoring is warranted unless there are overwhelming reasons to believe the accused represents a grave danger to the public and thus needs to be temporarily incapacitated. Given that the U.S. system of criminal law is not entirely fair, there is even stronger reason to abandon bail as a mechanism of accountability.

Prison, Privatization, and Profit

One way to argue for the abolition of the prison industrial complex is to focus critical attention, not so much on prisons, but on capitalism. For instance, the critic of the prison industrial complex could argue that capitalism is an oppressive social system— say, unjust, undemocratic, dehumanizing, or exploitative—and so its basic institutions (such as private ownership of productive assets, wage labor, markets, and private finance) should be dismantled and replaced. On anti-capitalist grounds, it would also be natural to oppose the prison industrial complex, as it necessarily relies on and is enmeshed with capitalist practices and products. In this way, there is a direct road from a critique of capitalism to the demand to abolish the prison industrial complex.

But this ground of opposition would apply to *many* institutions and organizations—not only prisons and the military but also schools, hospitals, banks, news organizations, communication networks, mass transportation, homes for the elderly, and even the family. The thesis that the prison industrial complex should be abolished would then just be a theorem derived from the more general claim that *capitalism* should be abolished. An institution that necessarily depends upon and operates through an inherently unjust practice could never be fully legitimate and would be morally tainted by its association with the oppressive practice. Prisons wouldn't be special in that regard; and the primary critical task would be to convince skeptics that no form of capitalism is compatible with true human freedom—which, on one plausible interpretation, was Marx's aim in *Capital*.

Yet Davis and other abolitionists have objections to the prison industrial complex apart from their general objections to capitalism. They are also concerned with how prisons interact with or are shaped by capitalism, and these concerns will be my focus. To isolate these specific worries, keeping them distinct from opposition to capitalism itself, I shall assume that capitalism is not inherently unjust. To be clear, I am not assuming that *existing* capitalist practices are just, far from it. I assume only—and here primarily for the sake of argument—that there is a realistic form of capitalism that would be compatible with a stable, just, and democratic society.

To gain further clarity about what, morally speaking, is at issue, we need to make explicit the meaning of some relevant terms. *Privatization* is the process by which a property or enterprise goes from being government owned (or publicly owned) to being privately owned. Privatization can involve two types of rights transfer: the transfer of *ownership rights* to assets (such as land, facilities, vehicles, or machinery) and the transfer of *operating rights* to an enterprise (say, the prerogative to provide certain goods or services). Sometimes a public function (for instance, law enforcement, education, transportation, or sanitation) is carried out, at least in part, by a private organization rather than a government agency or public-service employees. This *outsourcing* arrangement is facilitated by public-private contracts and needn't involve the transfer of ownership rights. Public institutions also often make use of *private suppliers* for goods and resources needed to carry out relevant public functions, but without turning over any ownership or operating rights.

Private organizations can be for-profit or nonprofit. *Profit* is a financial benefit that is realized when the amount of revenue gained from a business enterprise exceeds the costs (including taxes) needed to sustain the enterprise. The primary purpose or goal of for-profit organizations is to secure profit. If we rely on capitalist principles, any profit that is gained through the enterprise belongs to the business's owners, who are free to decide what to spend it on (for example, reinvestment in the enterprise, stocks or bonds, personal consumption, donation, and lobbying) and free to save it for future use.

A nonprofit private organization exists for purposes other than generating profit, such as serving a community, advancing a cause, or benefiting the general public. Although the organization's members may be concerned with revenue, costs, debts, and efficiency, they are concerned about these financial matters only insofar as they bear on keeping the organization operating, expanding it, or making it operate better. Members of a non-profit do not own stock in the organization and thus have no claim on financial benefits based on ownership rights. Nonprofits are also often (though not always) mission-driven, and therefore make decisions to advance their mission on grounds which their for-profit counterparts may not take into account.

Labor compensation is different from profit. Although both can serve as motives and rewards, labor compensation is a financial benefit derived from providing a service or doing some task. It is payment in exchange for actual work. Such payment can be given to a public-service employee working for a government agency or to an employee working for a private organization (profit or nonprofit). Employees are free to decide what to spend their compensation on (for instance, stock, consumption, gifts, lobbying, and so on) and may save it for future use. The distinction between commercial profit and labor compensation is meant to mark the difference between deriving a financial benefit from *ownership* and deriving it from *work*.

With these distinctions in mind, we can more readily see that objections to the prison industrial complex can take a variety of forms. I leave aside objections on grounds of cost-effectiveness and focus on moral objections. For instance, a concern could be that some private organizations are wrongly earning profit from prisons. Or the objection might be to granting administrative power over prisoners to private organizations. Or perhaps the issue is which specific prison functions are being outsourced to the private sector. Or the concern may be over ownership rights, which is its own form of power, a type of power that, when it comes to prisons, is perhaps only legitimately held by the public.

Corruption, Wrongful Gain,
and Perverse Incentives

Again, I assume, with Davis, that *retribution* for wrongdoing is not a legitimate public function. That is, I won't rely on the premise that those who commit crimes *deserve* to suffer and that the state has the rightful authority to use incarceration to ensure they endure this suffering. But on one influential view, and the one I favor, the official function or principal purpose of prisons (like other law-enforcement institutions) is to provide security to the public by preventing and controlling crime—that is, by keeping crime within tolerable levels so that everyone's basic liberties and rightful possessions are adequately secured. The provision of this essential public good is a fundamental state responsibility. Indeed, on some accounts, it is the primary justification for governmental authority and for the state's claim on a monopoly over the use of coercion.

Davis claims, however, that for-profit companies in the prison industry do not actually seek to provide security but only to make money for shareholders. The real or latent function of these institutions is to amass private wealth under the ideological cover of providing a necessary public good.[4] Prison privatization is, in effect, a *scam*—a way to accumulate private capital using public funds (and sometimes using prison labor) and on the pretext of making an essential contribution to public safety.

This critique reaches beyond the familiar charge that capitalists are greedy and indifferent to the human costs of their enterprises. It is an objection to neoliberal governance, in particular to public-private contracts to carry out public functions. Governments make contracts with private companies in prison-related industries. Presumably, these contracts would not be renewed unless government officials were satisfied with the services provided (assuming there is sufficient competition for government contracts). This suggests that these officials (and perhaps the institutions of which they are a part) are *corrupt,* that they are colluding with businesses that profit from public revenue without providing the relevant public good. For-profit companies often engage in lobbying efforts that exacerbate the problem of corruption among public officials. They also sometimes participate in misinformation campaigns to mislead the public and thereby sway it in their favor. I have no doubt about the reality or seriousness of these problems of corruption. Yet here authorities clearly *misuse* carceral institutions and *abuse* their power to make and implement crime-control policies. Something similar happens in the arenas of education, health care, and housing.

However, a similar form of corruption can occur within a wholly public prison system. Public officials, too, can be indifferent to whether prisons help to secure public safety. Their chief concern is sometimes keeping their jobs (along with the compensation, power, and status attached to their positions). And it is not just high-level public officials who have motives that could undermine public functions. Lower-level public-service employees may be similarly motivated. For instance, prison-guard unions have a financial stake in keeping prisons open and full regardless of whether this would prevent crime or rehabilitate prisoners. Consequently, they may be tempted to defend the need for draconian sentences. They also have an incentive to resist managerial or technological innovations that would ease the burdens on prisoners but reduce the need for correctional officers.

Unfortunately, the broader public often fails to check these abuses. Citizens might not hold these officials and public employees accountable for their poor performance and unethical conduct because they lack the power to do anything about it, or because they don't know about the corruption, or because they are insufficiently concerned about the problem, perhaps because they lack sympathy for those convicted of felonies.

The vice of being indifferent to whether a public good is adequately provided can afflict public institutions and private organizations. Whenever it is possible to continue acquiring benefits regardless of the quality of the goods or services provided, we should not be surprised if some fail to carry out these responsibilities in good faith and in a conscientious way. Private organizations hardly have a monopoly on institutional corruption. Such corruption should be exposed and ended, which requires being vigilant in both the public and the private sector.

But let's suppose the relevant private organizations actually provide adequate services and products in a cost-effective way. Would the fact that profit is their motive and reward be sufficient reason to prohibit the practice of privatizing prisons? Davis thinks so, and for two reasons. She objects to the *source* of these profits, namely, the intentional deprivation of freedom and imposition of hardships on prisoners and their families. She also thinks that the *profit motive* undermines the effective provision of public goods (in this case, security) and is a strong incentive to maintain horrid prison conditions (as a cost-cutting measure to maximize profit).

The first concern—the unsavory source of profit—suggests that the relevant principle is that *no one should gain financially from the suffering caused by imprisonment.* Yet even if prisons were constructed, maintained, and administered solely by public-service employees, these employees' labor would be (and should be) compensated and so they would gain financially from the suffering of inmates and their loved ones.

Perhaps the objection is not to fair compensation for necessary work but rather to profiting from ownership of prison-industry firms. The distinction between profit and labor compensation doesn't appear to help, though, because at least some financial gain from property rights would appear to be permissible in this domain. For example, prisons need supplies and resources— food, clothes, bedding, medical supplies, equipment, technology, toiletries, fuel, and so on—that, in a capitalist society, will be provided, at least partially, by for-profit organizations. The owners or shareholders of these companies will therefore profit from prisoners' suffering and curtailed freedom. Indeed, incarceration makes capital gains possible for at least some employees of public prisons, for they (at least the more highly paid among them) can use a portion of their pay to buy shares in companies, and this ownership may yield financial benefits. Although somewhat indirect, this too would be profiting from the suffering caused by incarceration.

A slightly different underlying principle is this: *No one should profit from the harmful wrongdoing of others,* in this case, from the serious crimes of prisoners. Again, this is overly broad, and for the same reasons as before. Medical personnel and hospitals do no wrong when they expect to be paid for treating victims of serious crimes. And a private company reasonably expects to turn a profit from the sale of its goods and services used in such medical treatment.

It could be maintained that one is permitted to profit from others' harmful wrongdoing but *only if in so doing one also contributes to repairing the harm, redressing the wrong, or preventing further such wrongdoing.* This might explain the moral acceptability of the medical case. But a private prison that contains convicted serious offenders will usually satisfy this condition as well.

A sounder principle would be something like this: *One should not seek to profit from suffering caused by injustices one has perpetrated.* In other words, it is wrong to act so as to profit from one's *own* harmful wrongdoing. One might inadvertently profit from a wrong one has committed, but one may not act wrongly so as to profit from the wrong. This is widely and rightly regarded as impermissible. I believe Davis is on firm ground here.[5] To the extent that a corporation is blameworthy for creating or perpetuating crime, it should not turn this wrongdoing to its advantage by profiting from prisons. I will return to this point.

Davis's second concern with profit from prisons is that it creates *perverse incentives*—namely, practical reasons to lock up people and to impose long sentences even when this won't prevent crime.[6] It is a morally unacceptable situation when there exist operative reasons to impose unnecessary suffering. In response to this legitimate worry, reformers could insist that arrests, indictments, verdicts, sentencing, parole, and release decisions be made only by those without a financial stake in the outcome of those decisions (and perhaps who can't be hired or fired by someone with such a stake). They might also maintain that government officials who regulate or oversee the prison industry should be prevented from having a financial stake in that industry. These reform efforts would be directed toward reducing conflicts of interest between actors in prison-related firms and the aim of fair and humane crime prevention. No reasonable and honest defender of prison privatization believes that the corrections industry should be free to operate without public oversight and government regulations.

This response, however, is not entirely adequate, as the problem runs deeper. There is in fact a second perverse incentive: to keep the costs of prison administration as low as possible so as to increase profits. This incentive can lead to limiting or cutting educational, vocational, health care, psychiatric, or rehabilitation services. It can lead to unsanitary environmental conditions, low-quality or unhealthy food, and prisoner overcrowding. It can lead to reducing correctional staff to dangerously low levels or to hiring the cheapest workers available without due regard for their competence and commitment to doing the job well.

The cost-cutting problem can negatively affect the administration of public prisons, too. Public revenue is limited. Budgetary considerations (including public debt and deficits) can lead to the elimination of valuable prison programs and the hiring of inadequate staff. And the public, given its usual contempt for prisoners and embrace of retributive attitudes, may not support greater spending or higher taxes to improve the lives and safety of prisoners, thus placing a democratic constraint on what public officials may do to improve prisons. So the incentive to keep costs down (whether to increase profit margins or to stay within budgetary constraints) is powerful and present for public and private organizations.

However, the incentive to cut costs, even for vital goods and services, is *inherent* in for-profit enterprises. There is no way to eliminate it. The public can only try through government oversight and regulation to prevent corporations from acting on the incentive in ways that compromise the provision of adequate public goods and services. By contrast, the public could be convinced—on grounds of justice, human rights, or public safety—to spend more money on prisons and prison services. This is one reason to prefer public prisons over privatized for-profit prisons.

There is another reason to prefer public prisons over privatized for-profit prisons. Not only do for-profit private prisons have no incentive to rehabilitate prisoners or to reduce recidivism. They have an incentive to *promote* crime and criminality. Creating prison conditions that make prisoners more likely to reoffend once released or more likely to violate prison rules that extend their prison stay is actually good for business. Insofar as for-profit prisons exacerbate the crime problem in this way, they profit from suffering caused by their own unjust actions. (Recall our earlier principle: *One should not seek to profit from suffering caused by injustices one has perpetrated.*) The injustices at issue are encouraging criminal activity and complicity in any subsequent crime. The temptation to engage in such wrongdoing might be so strong and the resulting harms so enormous that it would be better not to run the risk of using for-profit private prisons. The general public is not subject to such temptation. It seeks cost-effective ways to limit crime. Efficient crime control means not only greater public safety but also more public resources for things like schools, hospitals, and parks.

It could be argued that the problem is not so much profiting from prison ownership or prison administration as it is profiting from prison *labor*. Private companies do sometimes contract with the state to gain access to cheap prison labor (whether in a public or private prison). Yet where inmates can refuse to work for private companies without incurring penalty, the fact that a private company profits from prison labor isn't in itself unjust—*unless capitalism is unjust*. Many non-incarcerated persons, to meet their material needs, seek employment from for-profit companies that pay low wages.

Perhaps Marx was right that wage labor under capitalism is a form of slavery—dehumanizing servitude under despotic rule. But if so, prison labor that benefits private firms would be an instance of a much more widespread unjust practice that occurs inside and outside prison walls, not a distinctive form of oppression. And, again, our call should therefore be for the abolition of *capitalism*, not the abolition of prisons, except insofar as they are part of the capitalist system. In any case, profit can be secured from prisons without extracting it directly from prison labor.[7] Thus, ending prison labor or raising prisoner wages, though perhaps welcome on other grounds, will not abolish the prison industrial complex.

One motive for the privatization of a public function is to weaken organized labor, which keeps wages low. This is an objectionable way to reduce public expenses, for it leaves workers vulnerable to exploitation and wrongly reduces the value of their basic liberties. It is clear that government can save money by relying on private companies partly because these companies unfairly squeeze labor (including prohibiting or undermining unions). But reform seems possible here, too. Governments could get some of the advantages of agreements with private companies (for example, efficiency due to specialization and economies of scale) while only contracting the services of vendors with fair labor practices, including respecting the right of workers to organize and strike.

However, Davis opposes public prisons that rely on for-profit companies for *any* goods and services.[8] And she extends her critique to domains beyond law enforcement. She argues that there are certain vital public goods—security, education, shelter, and health care—that should be available to everyone on the basis of *need* alone and that providing these goods shouldn't depend on whether doing so would also turn a profit. Private for-profit companies should play no role in the provision of these public goods, on her account. Therefore, these public services, she argues, must be moved entirely to the public sector.

I find this idea appealing, yet it is difficult to see how a non-socialist government could ensure universal access to education, health care, and housing without extensive reliance on for-profit companies. Some of the personnel, supplies, technology, vehicles, and facilities needed to provide these goods and services would have to come from the for-profit private sector. Just consider what it takes to build and maintain a single high school—one or more buildings, hundreds of books, computers, desks, chairs, electricity, food, clean water, lab equipment, sporting equipment, art supplies, cleaning supplies, maintenance equipment, medical supplies, and so on. To avoid reliance on for-profit companies completely, the government would have to take over almost the entire economy just to ensure that all children have access to a decent school. At the very least, the government would have to enable, support, and rely exclusively upon nonprofit worker cooperatives. However, this would make Davis's opposition to privatization—whether of prisons or anything else—just a consequence of her opposition to capitalism. It wouldn't have to do with prisons per se.

Nonprofit Prison Privatization?

The critique of the prison industrial complex—again, when not simply a general expression of anti-capitalism—is best regarded as principled opposition to structural injustice. That is, it is concerned, not about privatization of carceral functions as such, but about privatization in the context of a wide range of serious social injustices, from economic and racial injustice to gender injustice and undemocratic practices. Under the current unjust background social conditions, a scheme of cooperation between the public penal system and the corporate world is deeply worrisome, even frightening. Such a collaboration has many perils that are difficult, if not impossible, to limit adequately through government regulation and public accountability measures. Moreover, the continuing reliance on for-profit private prisons is likely to further erode public trust in the criminal justice system, which needs to be widely accepted as legitimate if it is to be effective at crime control. To maintain or regain political legitimacy, justice in criminal law must not only be upheld but must be *seen* to be upheld. Transparency and accountability are crucial here, and commercial mechanisms and the profit motive can inhibit, if not undermine, these democratic ends.

Notice, however, that the choice is not limited to publicly owned, fully government-operated prisons or private for-profit prisons. There is also the possibility of a nonprofit private organization administering and perhaps owning a prison facility.[9] Prison privatization *without profit* could be a viable option under certain special, although not uncommon, circumstances.

Such an unusual and perhaps quixotic proposal immediately raises a few questions. First, how, practically speaking, would such an arrangement work? Second, why think this arrangement would be better, from a moral point of view, than the alternatives—public prisons, private for-profit prisons, or no prisons at all? And third, under what circumstances might this public-nonprofit arrangement be justified?

A well-funded private organization committed to protecting the interests of a vulnerable population or to promote the public good could make a contract with a government (local, state, or federal) to take over some core carceral functions.[10] Among these functions are ensuring prisoner safety (from others' aggression and self-harm), health care (including mental-health care), nutrition and physical fitness, maintenance and sanitation, prisoner supervision and perimeter security, discipline for prison-rule violations, facilitating in-person and remote interaction between prisoners and their families and friends, and educational and vocational services.

A nonprofit private incarceration facility could also be used to hold those charged with crimes but not yet convicted. Again, pretrial detention is overused, and bail is sometimes set too high and often completely unnecessary. But to the extent that such measures are needed to ensure accountability or incapacitation, private jails could be used when bail is denied, cannot be raised, or is refused by the accused. The private organization could be held responsible for custodial care and for ensuring that prisoners appear for trial. This would be functionally equivalent to holding a private entity financially liable (through forfeiting their bond payment) for when the accused fails to appear in court.

Some might object to permitting private agents to use coercion or violence against prisoners, insisting that the use of force should never be delegated from the public to a private actor. Let's assume this position is sound. It would not rule out nonprofit, private prison administration and services. The enforcement of a prison's perimeter (to prevent escape and unauthorized entry) and the use of force to ensure safety, order, and discipline could remain exclusively in the hands of state agents, that is, public employees trained and officially authorized to play this role. The remaining functions would be in the hands of a private organization and its employees and volunteers, subject of course to public rules and accountability. This would be similar to other private organizations (for example, private universities and hospitals) that rely on the police for certain purposes or under certain circumstances.

Now let's assume that some coercive functions can be legitimately outsourced or privatized. (After all, physical force *is* sometimes used in private psychiatric hospitals and schools.) To the extent that private security is relied upon, such personnel could be required to receive specialized and publicly approved training and to go through psychological evaluation and background checks. Perhaps all correctional officers in the private organization should be required to pass certain tests and to secure a license to serve in this capacity. This is already true of medical personnel who work in prisons (public or private).

To reduce reliance on coercion and violence in the facility, it might be wise to permit only nonviolent offenders to be admitted to a private prison. Or prisoners convicted of violent crimes could be permitted but only if they are appropriate for a minimum-, low-, or perhaps medium-security prison. For example, some prisoners, convicted of violent crimes long ago, are now elderly or infirm and pose no risk to others. Or prisoners serving a sentence for a violent crime may have shown themselves to be no danger to other prisoners or prison staff. But all prisoners who, for reasons of custodial care or security, are best held in a maximum-security facility could be excluded from private prisons.

If the major administrative and service roles within the prison were undertaken by the nonprofit organization and the prison itself was owned either by the organization or the public, this would effectively eliminate the problems of wrongful financial profit and profit as a perverse incentive. The organization would not be in violation of the principle that no one should seek to profit from suffering caused by their own unjust acts, because it would not be seeking to profit from the enterprise at all. Neither those who own nor those who run the prison would have a right or duty to maximize profit or shareholder gains. Unlike the for-profit prison industry, nonprofit prisons would have no financial incentive to increase crime rates, recidivism, or societal punitiveness. They could concern themselves with money matters only insofar as this was necessary to ensure the continuance of the prison. They could carry out the entire operation at cost, folding any budget surplus into improving prison conditions, services, and administration.

To reduce the risk of impropriety and corruption, the private organization could have an all-volunteer board with no members who have a stake in prison-related industries. Paid staff could be kept to a minimum. Participation from affected communities could be encouraged or even required. Of course, it might be difficult for a nonprofit organization (or even a group of such organizations) to raise sufficient funds to build a prison facility, or to buy or rent the land on which a prison would sit.

However, the public could own the land and facilities and the prison could be operated (in whole or in part) by a private organization. The public-private arrangement would concern prison administration and services on public property, not prison construction or the renting of private property. This, too, should reduce concerns about intrusions from corporate actors and the corrupting influence of the profit motive.

A nonprofit private prison would secure part of its funding from the public and so would be subject to public accountability measures. But it would also secure some of its funding from private donations. This would enable concerned members of the community to help shape the leadership, goals, and operation of the institution, rather than relying exclusively on state bureaucracy and business interests. These private donors could, for example, aim to satisfy higher standards for custodial care than public prisons are required to. They could offer more or better services to prisoners, including educational, vocational, medical, drug-treatment, and reentry services.

For those deeply concerned about the plight of disadvantaged black, Latinx, and indigenous peoples in the United States (social groups who are disproportionately incarcerated) but skeptical that existing governments can be trusted to secure adequate custodial care for prisoners from these populations, this public-private arrangement could be an avenue for community control over central elements of law enforcement. It could also be a way to address unacceptable prison conditions. If this is correct, then some outsourcing of penal functions could be beneficial to the oppressed.

Those who call for affected communities to play a significant role in crime control, including civilian oversight of the police, cannot consistently maintain that law-enforcement functions, to be legitimate, must be carried out entirely by public-service employees. If unjustly disadvantaged communities are to be truly empowered in the criminal justice arena, then they must possess effective private organizations that can counteract abuses of state power and reduce institutional corruption. A nonprofit, justice-promoting organization that could win a bid to run a jail or prison could play this role.

In suggesting a role for private nonprofit prisons, I am *not* claiming that a just society would permit these public functions to be moved to the private sector. This is a tentative proposal for nonideal conditions—for the circumstances of *injustice*. When social conditions are grossly unjust and the state lacks legitimacy in the eyes of the most disadvantaged, private inter-ventions are sometimes justified, even required. Systemic state failure can necessitate aggressive actions from civil society. The argument that punishment, to be legitimate, must be imposed through the collective *agency* of the public and in *name* of the public and so administered solely by public-sector employees democratically authorized to play this role is not applicable under conditions of intolerable injustice.[11] Given that the state operates with a serious deficit of legitimacy, the question is what practical measures of crime control, whether public or private, can be justified to those affected by those measures, particularly those among the oppressed.

Consider bail-fund organizations, such as The Bail Project or the National Bail Fund Network hosted by The Community Justice Exchange. Perhaps in a just world, there would be no cash bail and pretrial detention would be used (if at all) solely for those who pose an immediate danger to the community. Or maybe an egalitarian social order would ensure that each person had sufficient financial reserves to cover any bail costs. But in our highly unequal society, in which poverty is widespread and cash bail is set for even minor infractions, bail-fund organizations—which raise money from private donors to cover bail costs—play a vital if imperfect role for the disadvantaged, who would otherwise be stuck in jail until trial, often losing their jobs as a result, unable to care for dependents, and needlessly separated from family and friends. A nonprofit bail fund frees them from these burdens and makes such persons less likely to be exploited by for-profit bail-bond companies. More than this, though, such organizations could potentially save lives.

Consider the tragic case of Sandra Bland.[12] On July 10, 2015, Bland, a 28-year-old black woman, was pulled over for failing to signal a lane change. Texas state trooper Brian T. Encinia, a white man, got into an altercation with Bland after she refused to put out her cigarette and exit her vehicle. Encinia arrested Bland, charging her with assaulting a public servant, which is a felony. Bland was booked into the Waller County Jail in Hempstead, Texas, and her bail was set at $5000, though a $500 bond deposit would have secured her release. Bland asked family and friends for help but was unable to come up with the money. On July 13, just three days after her arrest, she was found dead in her cell, hanging from a noose formed from a trash bag. The death was ruled a suicide by medical examiners.

There are many troubling features of this case. Such a routine traffic stop should not have led to an arrest. There is the misconduct (and maybe the racism and sexism) of Officer Encinia, who was later indicted for perjury for falsely claiming that Bland had put his life in danger. Encinia also failed to de-escalate the

confrontation and, arguably, initiated it by arbitrarily demanding that Bland put out her cigarette. Given that Bland posed no
threat to others, there is a strong case to be made that she
should have been released without bail. But it's indisputable
that her life could have been saved with the help of a bail-fund
organization.

Bland's story also illustrates a failure of custodial care. During intake, she reported struggles with depression and that she
had once tried to kill herself after the death of her newborn. Yet
she was placed in a cell alone and not put on suicide watch.
Because of this institutional negligence, Bland's family filed a
wrongful-death lawsuit, which was settled in 2016 for $1.9 million.
In 2017, Texas enacted the Sandra Bland Act, which calls for
police training in de-escalation strategies, special protections
for those in custody who suffer from mental illness, and independent investigations of all prison deaths. Cases like Sandra Bland's reveal how nonprofit and justice-promoting
organizations could assist the disadvantaged not only through
bail funds but also by providing effective and caring prison
administration.

More generally, many in unjustly disadvantaged and racially
stigmatized communities need protection against wrongful
aggression and violence—murder, rape, and aggravated assault.
Some of the perpetrators of these wrongful harms are, tragi-
cally, themselves members of such communities. So, although
community members want these crimes prevented and highly
dangerous persons incapacitated, many (including some victims) are reluctant to hand over criminal offenders to a state
responsible for racialized mass incarceration and inhumane
prison facilities. In the right hands, nonprofit private prison

administration and services could be a viable, if temporary, alternative.

I don't know if the public-nonprofit arrangement I have described is *economically* feasible. It may be unrealistic to expect private actors, though trustworthy and genuinely concerned with the plight of prisoners, to be able to raise the necessary funds to operate a prison on a nonprofit basis. Perhaps any such nonprofit organization would be outbid by a for-profit firm. The arrangement could also be *politically* unfeasible, in the sense that there may be no practical path to taking away prison administration from the state or from public correctional officers' unions. Or perhaps there is no regulatory regime that can effectively monitor a private prison, whether for-profit or nonprofit. My aim here, though, has been merely to establish this principle: that the temporary, nonprofit privatization of central prison functions is morally defensible under nonideal conditions.

Acceptance of this principle is compatible with the abolitionist critique of the prison industrial complex, at least insofar as that critique does not rely on the premise that capitalism is inherently unjust. In addition, the principle is consistent with resistance to neoliberal governance, at least insofar as such objections are primarily to public contracts with for-profit companies and not to all public-private partnerships. Moreover, limited private nonprofit prison administration is, in principle, consistent with the fundamental aims of prison abolitionists. Few, if any, would insist that all prisoners should be immediately released and that there must be no new prisoners regardless of the risks or costs (what in the previous chapter I called a "radical moratorium" on prisons). A world without prisons, abolitionists insist, is a long-term goal that would require broad structural transformation before prisons are truly obsolete. In the meantime, some limited use of prisons is, regrettably, a necessary evil. Yet abolitionists don't trust the state to incarcerate in a way that is humane and safe and that treats prisoners with dignity. Nor do they trust the corporate world to fill the gap. A nonprofit private entity could be the best option and is in keeping with the spirit of creative experimentalism at the heart of the abolitionist ethos.

CHAPTER 5

Responding to Crime: Incarceration and Its Alternatives

For centuries, communities have used some form of punishment to penalize those who wrong others. Before the wide use of modern incarceration, these punishments were almost always unspeakably cruel and harsh, including execution, maiming, enslavement, torture, banishment, and severe beatings. And these practices still exist in some countries. Imprisonment is generally considered to be more humane and less brutal. But this comparative advantage is insufficient to justify the practice. Nor is the fact that prisons are present in every nation of the contemporary world a good reason to think their existence should, or needs to, continue. A practice that deprives people of basic freedoms and imposes other serious harms requires a deeper defense.

As I have emphasized, those who defend the practice of imprisonment must justify it by showing that prisons prevent or reduce crime. Many abolitionists, including Angela Davis, deny that prisons help to control crime. Indeed, part of what makes the functional critique of prisons so compelling (see Chapter 3) is that it relies on a simple and almost irresistible inference: since prisons have been around for so long but don't actually prevent crime, something other than crime prevention—another and perhaps nefarious function—must explain their persistence.

Prison abolitionists argue that the practice of imprisonment does not and, even with reforms, could not help to prevent serious crime. If I were convinced that this charge was true, I would advocate for prison abolition. Though I do not believe that imprisonment is inherently or incorrigibly dehumanizing, inhumane, despotic, racist, or exploitative (see Chapters 2–4), I do believe that it inevitably causes significant harm to prisoners and their families. Since I do not accept retribution as a defense of imprisonment, the harm that prisons cause can only be justified by the good that they do or, with suitable reforms, the good that they could do. Imposing incarceration on those who commit crimes is a severe response to even serious wrongdoing. To justify the practice, we must be reasonably confident not only that it treats the accused fairly (through due process measures) but that it actually helps to control crime.

However, even if prisons do prevent crime, or could be reformed so that they do, if there are less harmful crime-control measures that would be at least as effective, we should opt for those. Davis and other prison abolitionists have defended alternatives to prison that they believe are less violent and more efficacious. So I will also consider those alternatives and ask whether they are superior and could displace prisons.

Deterrence

In theory, prisons reduce crime in three ways. They may do so through *deterrence*, that is, through the threat of imprisonment, which discourages criminal wrongdoing by way of prudence or fear. They may do so through *incapacitation*—being physically prevented from committing crimes due to confinement and separation from the public. And they may do so through *rehabilitation*, via in-prison services and organized activities designed to turn prisoners away from crime and to enable them to live a crime-free existence once released.

With respect to deterrence, two important questions arise. First, does the general threat of prison deter? Second, does the unpleasant experience of incarceration lead former prisoners to commit fewer crimes than they otherwise would? I won't attempt to provide a comprehensive answer to these questions. These are largely complex empirical matters that philosophical analysis alone cannot settle. Philosophy can, however, help to frame the relevant moral and policy questions. It also has a role to play in interpreting the practical significance of pertinent empirical findings.

It is helpful to distinguish between two forms of deterrence: general and specific. General deterrence is the *threat* of penal sanctions for committing a crime, which provides an incentive to refrain from crime. This is the threat everyone in society is under when a practice of punitive incarceration exists. Its effectiveness is usually measured by comparing crime rates with imprisonment rates—for example, looking to see if crime declines as imprisonment rises. Specific deterrence is a matter of how the *experience* of imprisonment (the loss of basic freedoms and opportunities that others enjoy) provides a disincentive for prisoners to reoffend once released, and is usually measured by recidivism rates.

Deterrence, whether general or specific, is a function of the *likelihood* that an offender will be punished and the *severity* of the punishment. Or to be more precise, it is the *belief* in the high probability and severity of punishment that has the potential to deter. If the probability of being punished is perceived to be very low, then the penalty, even if severe, will not have much if any deterrent effect. If the penalty is not regarded as particularly unpleasant, then the penalty, no matter how certain, won't deter.

There is evidence that, at a certain level of severity, lengthy prison terms do not deter any more than shorter ones.[1] Given that we should impose no more suffering than is needed to keep crime within tolerable levels, this gives us reason to make American sentences shorter, probably considerably shorter, as they are in other parts of the world. In the United States, the extremely lengthy prison terms (sometimes thirty or more years) could be justified only on grounds of retribution, which I reject. Similarly, there is evidence that once the overall prison population reaches a certain per capita level, increasing incarceration has a negligible impact on further reducing crime rates and might even be counterproductive.[2] This is yet another reason to be deeply troubled by mass incarceration. Although the rate of imprisonment in the United States has gone down in recent years, the country still has the highest incarceration rate in the world (ahead of Russia and China), but far from the lowest crime rates.[3]

Sometimes when abolitionists claim that prisons do not reduce crime, they are best understood as asserting that *mass incarceration* does not reduce crime, a claim I would not dispute. Showing that dramatically increased punitiveness does not reduce crime is not, however, the same as showing that no amount of incarceration reduces crime. When philosophers ask whether imprisonment serves as general deterrence, we are asking whether fear of imprisonment prevents more crime than if we did not have the practice of punitive incarceration. We are not asking whether increasing the *severity* of carceral penalties (for instance, lengthening sentences) or the *likelihood* of imprisonment (for example, raising the probability of prison admission given an arrest) will reduce crime. Questions such as these presuppose that we already have the practice of imprisonment and, on this supposition, ask which law-enforcement and penal policies would be most effective. And, as I suspect, perhaps a less harsh and less aggressive approach to law enforcement would control crime better.[4] But this point, though important, does not go to the heart of the reform-versus-abolition question.

We can ask whether changes in a penal system alter the crime rate. For example, we can see whether increasing a sentence for a given type of crime reduces the incidence of crimes of that type. We can also see whether decreasing a sentence for a given type of crime increases the incidence of crimes of that type. But both questions are different from asking whether in the absence of a penal system crime rates would go up or down or stay the same. They are also different from asking whether, say, if incarceration were no longer a penalty for homicide, there would be more or fewer murders.

What we really need to know is whether there is an achievable and cost-effective prison system that would prevent more crime

than any non-carceral alternative. The comparison is not between different carceral regimes—say, between a more or less
punitive set of policies—but between a carceral regime and non-
carceral crime-control measures. Answering this question defini-
tively through empirical means is difficult if not impossible.

For instance, we cannot test directly for general deterrence
using a randomized experiment. The entire population of a
country is under the penal regime, that is, subject to criminal
law and its sanctions. There is no practical or ethical way to have
a treatment group that is not vulnerable to the penalty of incarceration and a control group that is under the threat (particularly where control/treatment group membership is randomly
assigned) so that we can compare the results of the experiment.
Perhaps, though, some ingenious experiment will be devised
that permits an indirect test of the hypothesis.

Historically, philosophers have fallen back on so-called
thought experiments. The traditional social contract tradition
in political thought—from Thomas Hobbes to Jean-Jacques
Rousseau—has asked us to imagine a "state of nature" (that is,
a social world without a state and thus without any formal
mechanisms of law enforcement). And they have concluded
that any rational person would rather live under the general
threat of punishment (even severe punishment) than live
without effective law enforcement. These speculative thought
experiments, though suggestive, are not fully persuasive. They
either presuppose a contested conception of human nature, or
invalidly generalize from introspection. But they do highlight
the fact, already noted, that one's position on abolition will
naturally depend on generalizations about what humans are
like or what they would be like under rather different social

conditions than currently prevail. I will return to this issue below and in Chapter 6.

Social scientists and criminologists disagree over whether severe prison terms deter serious crimes. However, "studies of police presence consistently find that putting more police officers on the street has a substantial deterrent effect on serious crime."[5] There is also strong evidence that the strategic and proactive deployment of police to crime "hot spots" reduces crime.[6] When policing deters, there is reason to think that part of what would-be offenders fear is being arrested, charged with a crime, and ultimately convicted and sent to prison. Fear of arrest alone probably plays some role, because being arrested generally carries stigma and can disrupt a person's plans. But the more frightening dimension of arrest is the prospect of incarceration. If so, then fear of police is, at least in part, fear of prison. Therefore, prison does have some deterrent effect, though only in conjunction with effective policing.

An analogous point can be made about surveillance. The monitoring of public space—not only by police but also by surveillance cameras, private security personnel, and ordinary citizens—has risen sharply over the last few decades. Such surveillance arguably deters through the threat of detection and capture, which increases the likelihood of conviction and thereby imprisonment. In general, increasing the certainty of punishment is a more effective crime-control measure than increasing the severity of punishment.

Yet there is at least one interpretation of these findings about police presence that suggests that fear of prison is not the underlying mechanism. Some may fear, not so much being arrested, but being subjected to police violence. The physical danger that these encounters with police pose could lead some (particularly disadvantaged African-American, Native American, and Latinx males) to avoid crime or even the appearance of criminal wrongdoing. Here the deterrent effect would be due to fear of *police* rather than fear of prison. Being subject to police brutality and excessive force is obviously a violation of basic civil rights. But if we look to societies where fear of police brutality is low or where police are mostly unarmed and we find a similar deterrent effect of proactive or place-based policing, then this should increase our confidence that this effect is largely due to fear of prison. And there is such evidence, including in places like the UK, Sweden, and Denmark.[7]

However, if policing does deter, this is both good and bad, at least in societies like the United States. It is good because it is a better outcome if would-be offenders do not actually commit crimes for fear of arrest than if they were to offend and then go to prison. General deterrence is better than specific deterrence and carceral incapacitation, at least from a moral point of view and possibly with respect to cost-effectiveness. Where general deterrence has been effective, harm from wrongdoing is averted and those tempted to offend are not harmed by incarceration. Potential victims get protection without sending anyone to prison. It is thus a general harm-reduction strategy. And effective policing may cost less than incarcerating people, which is enormously expensive. But even if efficacious policing would be more expensive, the moral benefits, in terms of the reduction in overall harm, could outweigh the financial costs.

On the other hand, police are too often a menace to black people (and other people of color) in the United States, particularly to those who live or work in deeply disadvantaged black neighborhoods.[8] In addition to worries about harm done through police violence, there is the concern that when police regularly harass, unfairly treat, or disrespect black people, this lowers the sense of legitimacy of criminal law in the eyes of many blacks, particularly those living in racially segregated and poor communities.[9] There is an increasing and enduring sense of distrust and hostility toward law enforcement, passed on over generations, due to a supposedly just institution regularly behaving unjustly. This loss of legitimacy weakens the power of criminal prohibitions to produce compliance, as the threat of sanctions works best when combined with general respect for the law and trust in law-enforcement officials.[10] Moreover, when people regard law-enforcement officials as illegitimate, they may refuse or be reluctant to cooperate with criminal investigations, thus lowering the probability that offenders will be caught or punished. So in addition to worries about police violence, with more police contact there is the concern that such contact will further erode trust in law enforcement. The violence and harassment that disadvantaged black people commonly experience at the hands of the police might even seem to warrant ending *policing*, which some scholars, organizers, and activists have called for.[11]

So, it seems we face a dilemma. If we rely heavily on police to prevent crime, we potentially expose black people to greater police violence and harassment (that is, if the harms of policing scale with the level of policing, which seems reasonable to assume). Yet if we dramatically reduce reliance on police, black people may be exposed to more crime, including serious crime like murder. Is there a way to get the general deterrent effect of policing while reducing black people's vulnerability to police violence and harassment?

The obvious answer is that prison reform and police reform must be combined. We need prisons to deter serious crime; however, imprisonment as a practice is unworkable without police. But we don't have to, nor should we, live with policing practices as they are. Procedurally fair policing is called for by constitutional requirements of due process, a basic liberty of all citizens. Fairer treatment from police can also reduce the incidence of police brutality and repair deficits in legitimacy. This is clearly a long-term solution, as is true of broader social-structural transformation. In the meantime, and considering the dangers that current policing practices pose, perhaps a moratorium on certain *forms* of policing is called for.

For instance, limits could be placed on the range of offenses for which police have discretion to arrest, say, by making only the most serious criminal charges arrestable offenses. Court orders might be required for lesser charges. Arrest quotas could be prohibited altogether, as they arguably create perverse incentives and threaten citizens' civil rights. The circumstances under which the police have a right to stop, question, search, or pursue suspects could also be strictly limited. Limits could be placed on the situations in which the police have the discretion to investigate suspicious persons or circumstances. The range of situations in which the police have a right, or are obliged, to come to a scene when called could be narrowed. There could be much greater reliance on social workers and mental-health professionals to deal with social problems rather than always turning to the police. These would be reform efforts to reduce direct interaction between police officers and black people.

Hot-spot policing must be based on the high incidence of serious crimes in the area or the volume of complaints from community members, not on the racial makeup of the neighborhood. This should be data-driven policing, and racial profiling must be prohibited and strongly discouraged.[12] Use-of-force rules and procedures could also be altered, with serious penalties for officers who fail to comply, including facing criminal prosecution. Rewards could be offered to officers who develop a reputation for showing restraint in the use of force and who are effective in de-escalating volatile situations. Certain uses of force (for example, chokeholds and other neck restraints) could be strictly prohibited, and the use of lethal force could be severely limited (for instance, clear directives for when an officer may possess, draw, point, or discharge a firearm). Such measures are of course far from perfect and are not a full solution to the problem. But if they or similar policies were widely instituted, this might allow disadvantaged black communities to gain the crime-prevention benefits of proactive and hot-spot policing while reducing their vulnerability to the harms of police misconduct.

In many places, including the United States, recidivism is high.[13] Many former prisoners, within only a few years or even months after release, are rearrested, convicted, or sent back to prison (whether for a new crime or parole violation). It could be that some who reoffend cannot be deterred by the general threat of imprisonment despite having had the personal experience of prison. But there is also evidence that imprisonment can have a *criminogenic* effect on some prisoners. This is worrisome and a possible problem for reformers. Yet even if existing prisons do foster crime to some extent, this might be correctable.

Prison conditions, prison administration, in-prison services and opportunities, and prison sentencing are all objects of social reform, which if successful could significantly reduce the criminogenic effects of prison. As already noted, prison conditions can be and often are horrid—overcrowding, insufficient and incompetent staff, overuse of isolation, violence and sexual assault, inadequate sanitation and nutrition, lack of medical and psychiatric care, and so on. Prison staff can be cruel, arbitrary, and despotic. In some prisons, gangs wield enormous power, keeping some prisoners tethered to street culture and its law-breaking ethos, while acculturating others who may have had less prior connection to such antisocial attitudes. Many prisons fail to offer prisoners the counseling services (such as cognitive-behavioral therapy) and educational or vocational and employment opportunities necessary to reenter society as equal participants. And, as noted earlier, prisoners are generally held in prison for far too long. These needlessly lengthy sentences enable the corrupting dimensions of prison life and culture to have a deeper imprint on the incarcerated.

Reentry and reintegration conditions in the wider society must also be objects of reform. When the formerly incarcerated try to regain equal status, they are often subject to pervasive discrimination and civic exclusion, which can encourage a return to crime, either out of economic necessity or social alienation.[14] Where a practice of imprisonment also makes clear to prisoners and former prisoners that the public takes *satisfaction* in their suffering, is *indifferent* to their mistreatment, and will *never* welcome them back into society on equal terms, high rates of reoffending are to be expected. But these wrongful practices and this unforgiving social attitude are not universal. Not all societies exhibit them.[15] So there is reason to be optimistic that the criminogenic effect of imprisonment can be reduced through effective reform efforts inside and outside prisons.

It is possible that some cannot be deterred from reoffending because of firsthand experience of prison, even when prison conditions are humane and reintegration into society is effectively facilitated. Prison as specific deterrence may be of limited value in controlling serious crime. If so, this suggests it should not be a primary aim of imprisonment. Indeed, heavy reliance on specific deterrence could invite efforts to make prison life especially grim or unpleasant and may encourage the abuse of prisoners. Given this danger, there is reason to make the experience of imprisonment largely a matter of enhancing prisoners' capacity to refrain from crime by offering in-prison services and opportunities for rehabilitation.

But skepticism about the value of specific deterrence leaves open the question of whether serious crime would occur in the absence of the general threat of imprisonment. Looking at recidivism rates will not answer that question. What we need to know is why the *law-abiding* do not commit crimes, and whether fear of prison plays any role in their compliance.

Most people don't seem inclined or tempted to engage in the most serious forms of wrongdoing. Such grossly immoral behavior holds no attraction for them. They may even be repelled by it, particularly interpersonal violence. Among those who might be so inclined or tempted, some may hold themselves in check through moral considerations alone. Recognizing that unprovoked aggression against others is wrong is sufficient to keep them from acting violently or otherwise violating others' basic rights. Others may comply simply because the law requires it and they respect the law. Those insufficiently moved by considerations of morality or legality may remain nonviolent to secure the approbation (or to avoid the enmity) of their fellows or their gods. Some might be adequately deterred through non-carceral sanctions, like fines, property confiscation, supervised probation, and community service.

Yet the concern remains that giving up on the general deterrence that prison seems to provide could encourage or enable harmful wrongdoing among the otherwise law-abiding. The disincentive of a prison term could be a useful motivational supplement for those with a sense of justice but a weak will. Or it might sober the mind when the heat of passion threatens to overwhelm. Consider the widespread and salient disposition to respond to being victimized with retaliation. Revenge is a powerful if ugly motive. The threat of prison for acting from vengeance could curtail such acts.

Part of the reason that prison might fail to deter effectively in places like the United States is that the background social conditions are so harsh and unyielding for some that risking prison is, or at least seems, rational (having a higher expected utility than remaining within the bounds of the law).[16] When there isn't much to lose (including social rewards and public esteem) because one is already living an unrelenting miserable existence, then facing prison is less scary, or one might engage in unlawful conduct in desperation despite the fear. This suggests that prison might deter more effectively under more just conditions. Or at least, we cannot conclude from the fact (if it is a fact) that prison does not deter under highly unjust conditions that it would not deter under more just social arrangements.

Ordinary experience would seem to confirm that other kinds of penalties can deter noncompliance with laws and other rules. Those who drive automobiles know the experience of trying to avoid getting a parking ticket or reducing one's speed after spotting a police car. It is also an obvious fact that many follow the directives of their employers, not simply out of contractual obligation, but also because they fear being fired and consequently losing needed income. It is hard to believe that some people obey their bosses for fear of losing their jobs but that no one, or hardly anyone, obeys the law, at least in part, for fear of going to prison, particularly when if you go to prison, you will almost certainly also lose your job, and you will have limited opportunities to earn money while in prison. This is true even for many who do not work regularly in the formal economy. Earning money in the informal economy or gray market is also quite limited in prison. So it is not just the loss of personal freedom and the separation from family and friends but also (though for most probably less significantly) the economic opportunity costs of imprisonment that can potentially deter.

Incapacitation

Let me turn briefly to incapacitation. Human beings share many traits in common but also differ in ways that can limit the overall effectiveness of general deterrence. Some people enjoy taking risks—with their money, relationships, freedom, bodies, and lives. For some, the fact that they could go to prison for engaging in an illicit activity might be part of the thrill, even if they later regret the gamble. Some people are so myopic and present-oriented that they discount the future costs of their actions.

Some are intensely driven by passion, glory, or ideology and so disregard the risks associated with their actions. I highlight these obvious differences among human beings not to disparage anyone. These are normal and well-known variances in human personality that law-enforcement policy must take into account.

No society can bring the probability of punishment for a crime to a hundred percent. We generally cannot impose penalties immediately upon offense—criminal investigations and due process take time. We cannot eradicate all forms of irrationality, improvidence, and weakness of will. Therefore, we should not be surprised that, perhaps despite our best efforts, some people will not be deterred from committing crimes, even serious ones. But those who are risk-neutral or risk-averse and whose actions generally track their judgments *can* be deterred through formal sanctions. And those who cannot be deterred and refuse to turn away from serious crimes must sometimes be incapacitated through incarceration, at least temporarily, to protect others from grave harm.

It might seem unfair to imprison those who can't be deterred by the threat of incarceration. Perhaps it is not their fault that they have personality traits or habits of mind that make them impervious to credible threats. Why should they be made to suffer because they possess these characteristics? The social benefits might not seem sufficient justification to impose such suffering on persons who are unmoved by the threat of carceral sanctions.

Although they may not be at fault for being the kind of person who does not rationally heed credible threats, they might nonetheless be blameworthy for committing serious crimes. People should not be punished because they fail to heed the threat of incarceration. They should be punished because of their wrongful actions. When it comes to criminal law, it is the refusal to respect key moral requirements that is the main problem, not people's personality traits or their attitudes toward risk. We all have a responsibility to refrain from murder and rape even if we are strongly tempted to commit such terrible acts and even if we are attracted to danger. The severe penal response that incarceration represents would not be justified if the harms potentially averted were relatively minor. But this coercive response is sometimes warranted when it comes to serious crimes because of the vital interests at stake.

To be clear, I don't have in mind people who suffer from serious mental illness or who have severe cognitive or emotional disorders. When such people commit serious crimes, the response, if necessary, should be treatment in a psychiatric hospital, not imprisonment. I am talking about people who *can* comply with these moral and legal requirements but who find it more challenging to remain in compliance with them than the average person does. These outliers are certainly owed due process before any sanctions are imposed. But they are not wronged if sanctions are imposed despite their finding it more difficult than others not to succumb to temptation.

Consider men and women. As a generalization, it appears that adult males find it more difficult to resist aggressive and antisocial impulses than adult females. (In the United States, for example, the male prison population is roughly 93 percent of the total prison population. Similar numbers are found in the United Kingdom.) The fact (if it is a fact) that men find it harder to refrain from willfully harming others than do women would not, I take it, mean that men should not face prison for their harmful wrongdoing. (I leave aside whether individual sentences should vary by how difficult it was for the perpetrator to comply with the relevant law.[17])

In general, I doubt that would-be offenders are owed an incentive to refrain from such serious wrongs. The public owes the disincentive of imprisonment to people who are vulnerable to victimization. We should maintain a penal regime for purposes of public safety, to discourage and prevent criminal conduct within the general population. These penalties are a prudent concession to the unfortunate reality that some among us—not just monsters or predators but ordinary people—can be expected to act wrongly in the absence of sanctions. Would-be offenders do not all have the same opportunity to avoid these penalties. They do, however, have *sufficient* opportunity to avoid them. They can refrain (though perhaps not without difficulty) from actions that they have no right to engage in, that they have overriding moral reasons not to perform, and that cause others great and irreparable harm or deep and lasting trauma.

Our basic conception of human beings as rational agents who respond to incentives and disincentives gives us theoretical reasons for thinking that prisons reduce crime through general deterrence. There is also, as discussed earlier, empirical evidence that prisons prevent crime. These theoretical considerations and this empirical evidence are, to my mind, compelling. However, I can see why some might not find them fully convincing, and there is no consensus among social scientists and psychologists who study the matter. This fact—that there is room for reasonable doubt about whether prisons prevent crime—may be the strongest argument in favor of abolition.

Here, prison abolitionists draw our attention to a possible weakness in our penal system that reformers should take seriously. Yet we still need to ask whether non-carceral alternatives would fare any better.

Instead of Prisons?

In addition to advocating for a more egalitarian, less individualistic, and more democratic society, abolitionists like Angela Davis generally recommend four measures to deal with violent and other serious crimes. We should, first, make mental-health care available to all. Justice already requires this. But such medical services could also prevent crimes that wouldn't occur if not for untreated mental illness. Second, all should have access to affordable treatment for substance use disorders and drug addiction. Third, we should make stronger efforts to rehabilitate those who commit criminal offenses. Finally, we should employ reparative or restorative justice measures, as mechanisms of accountability, to reconcile offenders with their victims and to undo, or compensate for, the harm done.

I strongly endorse all four measures. Using them, particularly in combination, would significantly reduce the problem of crime. Yet I would argue that we should use these measures, not instead of prisons, but, at least sometimes, in conjunction with incarceration. None of these proposed abolitionist measures are incompatible with punitive incarceration, and imprisonment could be a useful and justifiable supplement to them. In fact, I believe that some of these measures are more likely to be effective if joined with the threat of prison or temporary carceral incapacitation.

Some persons with mental-health disabilities or psychological disorders commit crimes including serious offenses. The public should certainly offer, facilitate, and subsidize the therapy and medication necessary to heal or assist those suffering from debilitating psychological maladies. This help should extend to those who have known challenges managing their anger or who otherwise find it difficult to refrain from acting on aggressive impulses. There are, however, at least two limitations to relying on mental-health care to control crime if doing so would mean altogether abandoning incarceration.

The first is that some persons with mental illnesses are, because of their maladies, a danger to others. To protect the vulnerable, these dangerous individuals must sometimes be incarcerated (a form of incapacitation) while they undergo treatment. When appropriately conceived and carried out, this kind of incarceration should not be considered punishment, as these individuals either have not committed a crime or are not responsible for any crimes they have committed. Although an added purpose of this incarceration (medical care) would be different from the sole aim of imprisonment (crime prevention), from the perspective of those confined, the two forms of incarceration might still look and feel much the same. Both would inevitably involve severe restrictions on liberty and loss of privacy, and both would generally cause significant emotional distress. The main difference would be that the mentally ill would be released once they no longer posed a danger to others, while at least some criminal offenders would remain incarcerated until they served their full sentence.

It is true that a prison abolitionist could consistently allow the involuntary incarceration of persons who are mentally ill and clearly dangerous. Davis, for example, favors the abolition of prisons and penitentiaries but, so far as I can tell, is not opposed to psychiatric hospitals, at least not in principle. It is the *punitive* character of some incarceration that she is against. I think this response—distinguishing punitive from nonpunitive incarceration—has some power, but mainly against a conception of penalties as retribution. When the penalties are not conceived as retaliation or deserved suffering but serve only to prevent crime, they function similarly to involuntary commitment to a psychiatric hospital.

The other limitation of mental-health care as a crime-control measure is the need to respect personal liberty, specifically the right to not seek treatment. Some with known or suspected mental illnesses refuse to be treated or even diagnosed. There are those who initially accept treatment but then don't show up for therapy or won't take prescribed medication according to protocol. Such persons sometimes act aggressively toward others but could perhaps be effectively deterred by the threat of incarceration, either in a prison or a mental-health facility. After all, many who suffer from psychological disorders are not so debilitated that they are incapable of responding effectively to moral or prudential reasons. And some with mental illnesses are not without rational agency or a sense of justice and can therefore be held responsible for their wrongful actions (though they may be less culpable than those who lack such mental challenges). Respecting their freedom to refuse treatment while also protecting third parties from violent crime might require reliance on incarceration.

A similar limitation arises with therapeutic remedies for problems of drug use. Free treatment for drug use disorders and decriminalizing drug use would likely reduce crime.[18] But we can expect there to be some who refuse treatment and go on to commit serious crimes. Many won't seek treatment for their addiction or won't take prescribed medication, and some of these persons may commit crimes to feed their habit, or act violently under the influence of a drug.

Davis and other abolitionists favor rehabilitation as a response to criminal offending.[19] Yet they don't believe such rehabilitation can be effectively carried out in a prison. Davis argues that prisons make prisoners violent (or more violent) and thus they are obstacles to (rather than instruments of) rehabilitation.[20] She also suggests that effective rehabilitation will occur only when offenders can exercise their basic freedoms rather than being deprived of them.[21]

If prisons, no matter how they are structured or administered, make the imprisoned unsuitable to rejoin society as equal and non-violent participants, this would be a tremendous strike against imprisonment as a crime-control measure. Prisons would then create worse human beings and thereby contribute to a problem they are ostensibly meant to solve or mitigate. If it can be shown, with convincing empirical evidence including comparative studies, that prisons inevitably have these deleterious effects, the case for abolishing prisons would be powerful indeed.

But must imprisonment inevitably make prisoners violent or more violent? Much depends on whether prisoners would be isolated from one another, preventing human bonds from forming or being maintained. "Supermax" prisons, which keep prisoners in solitary confinement for up to twenty-three hours a day, are particularly troubling in this regard. Again, it would also depend on the length of prison sentences, which many reformers believe should be far shorter than they typically are. Moreover, prisoners need real opportunities to stay in contact with family and friends through regular in-person visits, phone calls (with video when feasible), and letters. This worry about psychological trauma might be another reason to enable and encourage prisoners to work when such work involves significant cooperation or social interaction (see Chapter 2).

Successful rehabilitation and reentry do hinge on prisoners having real opportunities to exercise many of their basic liberties. I argued in Chapter 2 that prisoners should retain as many of their rights and opportunities as is compatible with fair sentencing and custodial care. This would mean participating in public affairs, including exercising free-speech and voting rights. It would also mean having access to education and job training. And it would mean having opportunities to work and to earn and save money.

We must also allow for the possibility that, perhaps in rare cases, mental-health care, treatment for drug use problems, or rehabilitation would be most effective in the context of involuntary institutional confinement. Such drastic and coercive measures are probably not justifiable on paternalistic grounds alone (unless a minor is involved). But when those subject to incarceration have committed serious crimes, the justification is in part based on the need to secure public safety. Even where criminal offenders are offered mental-health services, help with drug problems, and rehabilitative programs, the threat of imprisonment may be necessary to ensure adequate participation and program compliance. Otherwise, not only would the public remain vulnerable to new offenses, but offenders won't get the help they need.

As I emphasized at the start, I strongly favor using non-carceral penalties to control crime where feasible and effective. Yet some lesser penalties, such as community service and home confinement, are difficult to enforce without the threat of incarceration for noncompliance. There's a sense in which prison, even if rarely used, anchors the entire scheme of penalties. Without it, society has few formal means to enforce its laws, mainly fines and the suspension of privileges, which are unlikely to be effective against serious crimes, such as rape and murder.[22]

Transformative Justice

Reparative justice and restorative justice aim to support victims, promote healing, compensate for harm done, and facilitate reconciliation. With reparative justice, the point is not simply to repair the harm, though this is critically important. The goal is also to set things right between the wrongdoer and the wronged and thereby resolve a legitimate grievance. With restorative justice, the call is to go beyond seeking closure and repairing harms (psychological, physical, or material) toward restoring relationships between people that have been broken or damaged due to injustice. Where the wrongdoer and the person wronged had no prior relationship, a new relationship is created by the wrong itself, a relationship with enmity or fear at its core. When successful, restorative justice measures bring about genuine reconciliation between victims and those who have wronged them.

Reparative and restorative justice are sometimes treated as components of the broader idea of *transformative justice* (sometimes called "community accountability"), which is a conception of justice that rejects the notion of "criminal justice" altogether and that refuses to rely on punitive incarceration or the police.[23] It is conceived as a mutually exclusive alternative to criminal law and its enforcement. Indeed, abolitionist advocates of transformative justice do not even use the language of criminal law—for example, "crime," "illegal," "offender," and "felon"—but instead favor the less stigmatizing language of "harm" and "persons who have harmed others." The focus of transformative justice is threefold.

First and foremost, transformative justice aims to respond to interpersonal violence and harm by lovingly attending to the needs of survivors—those who are harmed, aggrieved, or otherwise negatively affected by harmful wrongdoing. Survivors need support, safety, and healing from their trauma and loss. To be made whole, survivors often want those who harmed them to publicly acknowledge their wrongs, to accept responsibility for the harm done, and to apologize and make amends. Criminal prosecution does not, and cannot, address these needs. The necessary practices of care and accountability can be cultivated and maintained by community-based nonprofit organizations and grassroots advocacy groups or through decentralized and informal social networks. Communities must be empowered to address wrongdoing among their members. These communal practices are to be rooted in dialogue and the goal of repairing harm, not in getting even or the desire to inflict further harm. They are to be inclusive, voluntary, and nonviolent. Examples include crisis intervention, counseling, mediation, mutual aid efforts, safe houses, de-escalation methods, and the provision of emergency services.

The second focus of transformative justice is preventing future harm by addressing the material circumstances (such as homelessness and lack of money) and power dynamics that give rise to harmful wrongdoing. Abolitionist organizers committed to transformative justice aim to change the local circumstances that ignite or fuel interpersonal aggression and violence but without relying on law enforcement. This would involve addressing food and housing insecurity, encouraging those addicted to drugs or alcohol to seek treatment, helping to resolve long-standing enmity between individuals or groups, instituting afterschool programs and extracurricular activities for youth, providing political education on sexism and sexual consent, and facilitating family counseling. Again, these programs are to be initiated and carried out by local nonprofit organizations, advocacy groups, or social networks with thick ties to the relevant community.

In addition to community-based measures to meet the needs of survivors and to prevent harm, a third focus of transformative justice is working through group solidarity and intergroup coalitions to bring about far-reaching social-structural change. Such social justice goals should include eliminating poverty, providing adequate education for all, reducing unemployment, equitably sharing wealth, and creating more democratic social relations. For abolitionists in the black radical tradition, this would mean ultimately abandoning welfare-state capitalism in favor of social democracy or socialism. Systemic injustice and economic inequality are drivers of violence, fraud, and theft, and so corrective justice can also dramatically reduce harmful wrongdoing without sending people to prison. Criminal law gives no serious attention to the underlying social causes of crime, and having a disadvantaged background is rarely treated as a legitimate excuse or even a mitigating factor for those who violate the law.

I welcome these approaches to harmful wrongdoing and to social-structural change. Reparative, restorative, and transformative justice practices should play a much larger role in responding to crime and interpersonal harm than they typically do. Abolitionists are correct that we should expand the range of practices we use to address harmful wrongdoing. We should embrace experimentation with transformative justice measures, especially given the limited effectiveness and narrow scope of current criminal law procedures. A wide array of strategies is required to respond effectively to crime, its causes, and its harmful consequences. Criminal law should not be our sole or even our primary approach.

As abolition feminists emphasize, transformative justice is often a fitting response to domestic, gender, and sexual violence. In these cases, support for survivors, reconciliation, and healing from trauma are paramount, and penalizing those who caused the harm is secondary or sometimes counterproductive. In the discourse of transformative justice, there is a rejection of the idea of "victims" in favor of "persons who have experienced harm" or "survivors." This is because thinking of oneself as a victim (rather than a survivor) can be disempowering, as if one were defined by the harmful act, and thus can inhibit reclaiming agency and moving past the injury and trauma. Those who have been wrongfully harmed often feel or suspect that they are partly at fault for what happened to them, and this sense of shared blame sometimes haunts survivors, leaving them with a deep sense of guilt and shame. Having the one who caused the harm take responsibility for it can itself therefore be healing. So

I wholeheartedly agree that criminal prosecution generally fails to fully address the vital needs of survivors. Other practices, including those of transformative justice, are better suited to this task. Often the survivors of harmful wrongdoing are searching for something other than (or at least in addition to) a criminal conviction and punishment for the guilty. And they should have it.

It is also true that criminal law is not well suited to address the underlying social conditions that fuel violence. Nor is it a proper instrument for altering the basic institutions of society or for redistributing resources on a societal scale. The role of criminal law is and should be limited; it must be supplemented by other less harmful practices and policies, and transformative justice measures should be among them. But the fact that this narrow instrument for responding to crime—that is, criminal law and its enforcement—fails to meet all the needs of survivors and is an inadequate means for structural transformation does not mean it cannot serve a vital social purpose or that it can be readily replaced.

The main limitation of transformative justice is that it depends on the willing participation of persons who have experienced harm and persons who harm. That it is a voluntary and nonviolent strategy to address harm is a great virtue. But we cannot always expect willing cooperation from the relevant parties. Sometimes a survivor will decline to participate in these reparative and restorative processes and may even refuse to send or permit a surrogate. Often survivors won't feel safe, and in fact won't be safe, if those who harmed them are effectively free to attack them again, particularly if the aggressors show no signs of remorse. Survivors and the broader public still need an effective mechanism to stop or inhibit those who mean others harm. Criminal justice procedures, though far from ideal, should be available to survivors whose assailants refuse to be held accountable and to survivors who are unwilling to participate in transformative justice practices.

When all goes well, transformative justice practices can prevent further acts of violence. Some reparative measures can have a secondary rehabilitative function, for instance. The person who caused harm may honestly repent and renounce any intention to commit future harm. Or they may find the process of reconciliation sufficiently healing that they no longer carry the motives or dispositions that initially led them to do wrong. Reparative and restorative justice can prevent harm if the apology is sincere and those who have done wrong regret their actions. When reparations are a part of restorative justice, the amends must be freely given with an acknowledgment and apology. This provides a contrast with reparative justice in a legal context. Material reparations need not always be given voluntarily to repair the harm done; for example, through successful litigation and court order, reparations could be paid to survivors of racist police violence. Legal authorities can extract restitution and reparations from an unwilling or unrepentant aggressor. This too can help survivors heal, for financial resources are often necessary for them to get the support they need. Law enforcement and reparative justice are not then incompatible, and they sometimes work better in tandem. We do not have to choose between them. Those who are sentenced to prison should make every effort to repair the damage done by their wrongdoing while in prison, once released, or both.

Another limitation of transformative justice is that neither reparative nor restorative justice can fully address the loss when a homicide has occurred. Reconciliation with the loved ones of a murder victim is not equivalent to reconciliation with the victim, whose lost life cannot be repaired or compensated. And persons who have killed another generally do not want their identities revealed and typically will evade accountability measures when possible. So, at least when it comes to murder, to rest the security of the vulnerable on transformative justice practices alone is to countenance enormous risk, which is one reason why I offer a qualified defense of strategies to deter and sometimes to incapacitate those strongly inclined or tempted to kill others.

Some abolitionists defend transformative justice as a challenge to criminal justice. I do not see why the two need be at odds. They are incompatible only if transformative justice requires a commitment to anarchism or unconditional pacifism, as discussed earlier (Chapter 2). They might appear to be opposed if the goal of criminal justice is thought to be retribution. But, as I have argued, the enforcement of criminal law is best understood as a public means for preventing and controlling crime. This goal is to be accomplished through general deterrence, rehabilitation, and, in exceptional cases, incapacitation.

It could be argued that transformative justice challenges the very idea that the enforcement of criminal law through imprisonment is, or ever could be, "justice." How could involuntary captivity and the suffering it inevitably causes constitute justice? But criminal law, when legitimate, is designed to protect our most basic liberties, including our right not to be killed, sexually assaulted, or physically attacked. Justice requires that these liberties be secure. They are secure only if people are reasonably protected against their violation. Otherwise, the liberties are merely formal and have limited practical value. Law that is unenforced provides no real protection for these vital interests. The general threat of legal sanctions contributes to such protection only if the threat is credible, which means the sanctions must be imposed when fair rules of due process warrant this. Justice is done, not because the guilty are made to suffer through confinement, but because criminal law procedures have worked as they should in maintaining a general practice of penal deterrence.

The Reality of Crime

Angela Davis ends her influential book *Are Prisons Obsolete?* with a moving story of reconciliation after a heinous crime.[24] In 1993, Amy Biehl, a white woman from California, was stoned and stabbed to death in a black township in Cape Town, South Africa. Four men were convicted of the crime and given an eighteen-year prison sentence. Remarkably, Biehl's parents supported the amnesty petition of the men, and they were released from prison in 1998 as part of South Africa's Truth and Reconciliation efforts. Restorative justice in this case required the victim's family to forgive the act that cost them the life of their daughter—forgiveness that they gave freely, and which enabled the perpetrators' redemption.

This kind of admirable and merciful action was perhaps necessary in the extraordinary circumstances of transitional justice after a long period of violent civil conflict in apartheid South

Africa. But is it reasonable to expect citizens to adopt this posture, as a general practice, toward people who try to kill them
or who murder those they love? This laudable disposition to
forgive might be acceptable for a religious group or an otherwise highly cohesive community. However, in a large, complex,
and pluralist society of people who are largely strangers to one
another, it strikes me as too much to ask if effective deterrents,
incapacitation, and rehabilitation are available to help control
such serious crime.

It is disappointing that the problem of serious crime is so
often dismissed, barely mentioned, or downplayed in abolitionist writings. Some claim that fear of crime is irrational or racist
and that people have more to fear from the police than from
so-called criminals. Or, as in the story just related from Davis,
violent crime is framed in the context of reparative and restorative justice. But once the problem is confronted forthrightly
and without the benefit of a conciliatory ending, the regrettable
need for prisons becomes harder to deny. A vivid and tragic
example may help to bring an element of realism to the discussion
and to make concrete how imprisonment can prevent irreparable harm.

Cynthia Glover, an African-American grandmother living
in New Orleans, has lost five close family members to gun
violence—three of her four children, her brother, and her grandson.[25] They were each killed in separate incidents in New
Orleans, though Glover believes that at least two were killed by
the same person. Her oldest son, Dwayne, was shot and killed,
just outside Cynthia's apartment, in 1997. He was only 18. No
one has been charged with his killing. Cynthia's only daughter,
Kendrell, was shot, just around the corner from Cynthia's

home, in 2013. Kendrell was 29. Cynthia's son Cornell was shot, again just outside her home, in 2014. (In 2019, a person was convicted and sentenced to thirty years for Cornell's murder and for attempting to kill Cornell's cousin Michael Glover three years earlier. As Cornell lay dying on the street from multiple gunshot wounds, he identified his assailant by name. A second gunman was never identified.[26]) Cynthia's grandson Dwayne ("Lil D") was also shot to death, a block from Cynthia's home, in 2017. He was nineteen. No one has been charged in connection with Dwayne's death.

Cynthia's only surviving and youngest son Alfred (who has also been shot on two separate occasions) is serving a ten-year prison sentence for possession of a firearm by a felon. (Cynthia says she brought the gun on a visit to Alfred's house but then forgot it there. It was later discovered by Alfred's parole officer.) Both Cynthia and Alfred are worried that he, too, will be killed. Cynthia now sleeps with a loaded 9mm handgun by her side. Her bed faces the front door of her apartment in case she needs to take quick action in self-defense. She has installed cameras outside and throughout her house in Algiers, a section of New Orleans.

The neighborhood that Cynthia Glover lives in and where she lost so many loved ones has an abysmally low arrest rate for homicides, with only two of twenty-three murders resulting in formal charges from 2010 to 2018. Low arrest rates allow murderers to remain menacing forces in the community, to act violently toward others without fear of going to prison. Low arrest rates also lead would-be offenders to believe they can take advantage of others and even kill them with impunity. The consequences can be devastating, as the Glover family learned. If some of the individuals who killed or wounded her children had faced punitive incarceration, even if only as a realistic threat, her life might not have been filled with so much unspeakable loss and perhaps she wouldn't be sleeping alongside a loaded gun.

I doubt that there are legitimate means that would prevent all serious crime. There will be no "end to crime." The most we can hope for is to minimize crime, to reduce it to a point where everyone has as much safety as anyone could reasonably expect and where constant fear of wrongful acts that do great and irreparable harm is irrational.

With serious crime a rare occurrence, it could be argued that the practice of imprisonment is indefensible. A just and good society would simply live with this small risk of harmful wrongs (perhaps making use of non-carceral penalties and transformative justice practices) rather than impose the suffering that prison causes. This approach to serious crime is even more plausible when we keep in mind that imprisonment harms not only prisoners but also those who care about or depend on them. So, one way of understanding Davis's alternative measures is to see them, not as eradicating all serious crime, but as bringing crime down to a level that imprisonment becomes too drastic a response to the problem.

But in those remaining occurrences of serious crime in the imagined prison-less society, what could the public say to victims? They could complain that had we established a credible general threat of imprisonment, their assailants may have refrained from attacking them. Or where an aggressor has seriously harmed others before, any new victims could rightly complain that the state should have incapacitated the individual (at least temporarily) to prevent harm to anyone else. The public could have taken perfectly permissible measures to avert this harmful wrongdoing but chose not to. Given that a primary responsibility of a legitimate state is to protect residents within its jurisdiction from unjust harm to their person, the state would be correctly seen as wronging the victims of crime.

CHAPTER 6

Dreaming Big: Utopian Imagination and Structural Transformation

This book began with the assumption that prison reform is needed, but sought to confront the challenge that reform is not a radical enough goal. We have thought through abolitionist criticisms of the practice of imprisonment, analyzed primarily through the leading work of Angela Davis. There is much in her wide-ranging critique of the prison industrial complex that is compelling and enhances the case for radical reform in existing prison systems, and law-enforcement practice more generally. Yet the case for the abolition of prisons is not wholly convincing. Incarceration has legitimate uses, including as punishment, at least when background structural conditions are reasonably just. The use of prisons to protect the vulnerable can sometimes even be justified in the context of systemic injustice.

Yet Davis's arguments for prison abolition are probing, insightful, and cannot be dismissed. Building on her rich work,

I offered considerations in favor of a limited moratorium on the use of prisons in the United States. We need to restrict our use of imprisonment to only the most serious offenses, the wrongs that do great and irreparable harm or cause deep and lasting trauma and which are wrong independently of whether the law prohibits them (*mala in se*). We should also dramatically shrink the current prison population, releasing those who have served long sentences and those whose crimes have not caused serious or irreparable harm.

In this concluding chapter, let me address possible abolitionist objections to my arguments in favor of prison reform. I also want to further distinguish the valuable utopian dimensions of abolitionist theory and practice from those that should be abandoned. And I will explain why even an extremely restricted use of prisons, which I believe is warranted in the United States today, must be combined with broader structural reform of society.

Abstraction, Idealization, and Counterfactuals

Some readers will have methodological concerns with my arguments. Many critical theorists and radical political philosophers are suspicious of so-called ideal theory and utopian reflection.[1] They worry that such theorizing abstracts away from concrete historical realities in a way that serves the status quo. Elsewhere I have defended my approach to political philosophy, in which both ideal theory and nonideal theory have an essential role.[2] That defense was offered largely within a liberal-egalitarian (or social-democratic) framework. Now let me explain how my approach is compatible with core commitments of Marxism and black radicalism.

Marx thought that the working class should, and would, abolish capitalism, at least eventually. Workers would do this by ending both private ownership of productive assets and markets in wage labor. Marx maintained that as long as capitalism continued, so would dehumanizing and despotic forms of involuntary servitude and also widespread poverty. He insisted that political subjugation, labor exploitation, and economic insecurity were *inherent* features of capitalism, not contingent characteristics of capitalist practice in this or that country or historical era. But to show that capitalism could not be reformed and must be abolished, he engaged in abstraction, idealization, and counterfactual reasoning. This kind of theorizing was politically wise and philosophically productive. Had he not engaged in it, opponents of socialism could plausibly respond to his critique by arguing that existing capitalism could be altered or improved upon to avoid the forms of oppression he identified. For instance, they could argue that instituting a generous welfare state, a living minimum wage, unemployment and retirement benefits, workplace protections for labor and a right to strike, a progressive tax scheme, and universal education and health care would adequately respond to Marx's most serious criticisms of capitalism.

Marx's analysis of the capitalist mode of production in terms of the surreptitious extraction of surplus value involves considerable abstraction from history and existing practice. He acknowledged that capitalism, as a matter of historical fact, arose and developed through "blood and fire"—that is, through violence, repressive laws, and the coercive expropriation of the peasantry.

As he tells us in *Capital*, "Thus were the agricultural folk first forcibly expropriated from the soil, driven from their homes, turned into vagabonds, and then whipped, branded and tortured by grotesquely terroristic laws into accepting the discipline necessary for the system of wage-labor."[3]

Yet Marx's critique of capitalism and his call for its abolition did not rest entirely on this damning historical analysis. Nor did he rely solely on the fact that direct force, corporate theft, illicit collusion among firms, and commercial fraud are commonplace in capitalist societies. He sought to show that even if markets operated without coercion, stealing, corruption, or swindling (as bourgeois ideology says they are supposed to), capital would still be concentrated in the hands of the few and the great majority would thus be at their mercy.

When I ask whether the practice of imprisonment should be reformed or abolished, I am engaging in a similar form of abstraction and idealization, and for the same reasons. I am not sugarcoating history or being evasive or naïve about grim concrete realities. My goal is to determine whether there are feasible changes that could be made now or in the future that would lead prisons to serve legitimate ends but without the forms of injustice that Davis and other abolitionists rightly condemn. The existing practice of imprisonment has deeply unsavory origins and operates, in many places, in a way that cannot be justified to prisoners and their families. But for abolition, in its radical form, to be compelling, skeptics will naturally want to know whether prisons would still be objectionable after realistic and suitable reforms.

When abolitionists claim prisons cannot be reformed, they could be saying that all (or most of) the changes that reformers have proposed were actually made and yet the same or similar problems persist and things have not substantially improved. Yet many of the proposed reforms I have discussed in this book have not been instituted, at least not universally and certainly not in the United States. In this way, the practice of imprisonment has the same status as the practice of socialism. In response to critics, defenders of socialism (like defenders of prisons) insist that there is a realistic form of socialism that departs in crucial ways from socialism as we have known it. This form of socialism would be democratic and stable and would meet everyone's needs in a reasonably efficient way while at the same time respecting individual liberty and freedom of expression. The socialist maintains that not all practical forms of socialism have been tried and that the history and existence of authoritarian and politically repressive socialist regimes does not show that realizing a just form of socialism is impossible.

Some radicals argue that *history* shows that prisons cannot be reformed. The record of failed reform efforts shows the project to be misguided because futile. This is not the same as saying that imprisonment, like slavery, is inherently unjust. Slavery cannot be "reformed," only abolished. But that is because it is intrinsically wrong. There is no form of slavery that could be justified to the enslaved. I have tried to show in previous chapters that punitive incarceration is not inherently unjust. The claim I am now considering is about what history (not moral reflection) can teach us. I have several questions about this use of history to establish abolitionist conclusions.

First, how are we to tell the difference between these two possible states of affairs?

(1) It is extremely difficult to reform practice X.
(2) Practice X cannot be reformed despite our best efforts.

The historical record can establish that (1) is the case. If serious, steadfast, and repeated reform efforts have been made in the past but few if any of these efforts were successful, then there is reason to conclude that (1) is true. Genuine social reform, particularly when fundamental change is sought, can be enormously challenging to achieve. But (1) can be true while (2) is false. The reform of educational institutions in the United States has been similarly arduous and protracted, and there is much work still to be done to make them fully inclusive, fair, and effective learning environments. Yet the difficulty of such reform is not a reason to believe it cannot be accomplished. We should expect that creating just institutions will be incredibly hard and that there will be numerous setbacks. The arc of the moral universe, as Martin Luther King Jr. has taught us, is indeed long, much longer than many of us would like. This fact does not counsel patience with injustice—"freedom now" should always be our demand—but it does suggest that we should be slow to reconsider our ideals when faced with recalcitrant and entrenched power.

Moreover, radicals should be wary of relying solely on a long record of failed political efforts to show that the goal of these efforts cannot be achieved. After all, various social movements have tried to make the United States a just society—a truly democratic, egalitarian, non-sexist, and non-racist society— since its founding, and have so far been unsuccessful. Why should we think the basic structure of U.S. society can be reformed (by, for example, moving away from a capitalist economy toward a socialist one) but that prisons cannot? Simply pointing to failed reform efforts in the past is not sufficient to establish the counterfactual claim that regardless of any social changes that could be made, no set of prison reforms could make imprisonment legitimate.

In addition, what historical grounds do we have to believe that it would be more challenging to reform prisons than to abolish them? If the opposition has thus far proved so powerful that it could successfully thwart all attempts at fundamental reform, why should history give us hope that an abolitionist movement, which involves contending with the same reactionary forces, would prevail? What is more, the political project of abolition is itself likely to be a protracted struggle, with many wrong turns and failures along the way, and with few major victories in the short term.

One could simply concede that, try as we might, we cannot feasibly abolish prisons, but insist that *if* we could do so, we should. Or reason and evidence could counsel us to expect the worst (that prisons will remain with us, at least for a very long time); but faith that good shall ultimately triumph over evil urges us to hope for the best (that one day, in the distant future, prisons will disappear). But these pessimistic conclusions or millenarian hopes are not what Davis and other like-minded activists believe. Their abolitionism is meant as a realistic and historically grounded political goal, something not only worth realizing and hoping for but that is realizable, through activism and organizing efforts, in the foreseeable future.

Finally, the prison reform initiatives that have been tried, we should remember, have occurred in a context of deep structural injustice. How do we know that, were we successful in making the background social structure more just, we could not (in that new context) fully reform the practice of imprisonment? I doubt that imprisonment could become a fully just practice when the wider social structure is profoundly marred by racism, misogyny, economic exploitation, imperialism, and poverty. But that does not mean that prison reform is impossible, only that our reform efforts should not be limited to improving prisons.

Utopian Reflection and Practice

I believe that radical abolitionism is utopian. This feature is, or can be, one of abolition's key virtues. Hopeful idealism and a willingness to call for fundamental social change are precisely what is needed in response to the enduring injustices, complacency, and cynicism that are so characteristic of our times. Yet utopianism is also, in other ways, among abolition's flaws, as I will explain. I begin with what makes utopian abolition valuable.

Angela Davis and other radical abolitionists oppose a "reform" framework because they believe it reinforces the ideological notion that prisons are a necessary and permanent feature of social life and prevents us from searching for and experimenting with alternatives.[4] I am not persuaded that prison reform is impossible or that prison abolition should be a central social justice objective. Yet I do believe abolitionists are correct that we should not treat prisons as inevitable or "natural" and that a search for alternatives is entirely worthwhile. Accordingly, one way of thinking about prison abolition is as a *framework for ethical reflection*.[5] We imagine a world without prisons and consider what attitudes, social relations, and institutions would be necessary to create and sustain that world. This is utopian thinking but in the good sense. It can allow us to gain a vantage point beyond ideological modes of thought, which function to reinforce social injustices.

By analogy, consider "poverty abolition." Rather than assume poverty will always be with us, we imagine a world without poverty, where everyone's basic needs are met. Regarding such a world as feasible can keep us from being complacent about the poverty that surrounds us. We should look beyond simply trying to "reduce" poverty or making it more bearable for those who suffer it. We then focus on constructing and experimenting with social arrangements that prioritize securing basic material well-being for everyone, without regarding our initial failures as establishing that this cannot be done. This utopian critical reflection is a healthy and potentially productive attitude to have toward prisons and poverty.

It is also crucial to contemporary socialist thought. Marx was extremely critical of utopian socialists who treated socialism as a set of ideals to be realized or who used moral arguments to effect radical social change. Marx's advocacy of socialism was, he insisted, rooted in a sober scientific analysis of capitalism and a materialist theory of historical development. Capitalism was to be abolished through militant and partisan class struggle, not through moral suasion or ordinary democratic channels. Nor did Marx do more than provide the barest sketch of a post-capitalist future.

Davis, though a former member of the Communist Party and deeply influenced by Marx, does root her socialist commitment in moral ideals like justice, freedom, community, and peace. She does not avoid moral appeals. Her case against capitalism is not grounded principally in historical materialism. Davis believes that capitalist societies are unjust, undemocratic, and needlessly violent, and these are the bases of her opposition. She also realizes that if her case is to be persuasive (even to members of the working class), she needs to give skeptics reason to believe an alternative social arrangement is within reach and would do a better job embodying the ideals she favors. The same is true of her advocacy of a world without prisons.

In other words, Davis recognizes the need to state not only what she is against but also what she is *for* and, just as important, to show how this vision can be realized using means that are morally permissible and at our disposal. Science, while increasing our *capacity* to effect dramatic change, cannot tell us what to value, what is worth fighting for, or which tactics are legitimate. History, though it too has its vital lessons to impart, does not exhaust the scope of the possible, provides no roadmap for the future, and guarantees no victories. Moral vision and dreams of freedom are critical resources.[6]

Abolitionist ethical reflection can demonstrate its practical value through community-based practices that prefigure, in an incremental way, a post-carceral future.[7] The abolitionist alternatives that Davis recommends—mental-health care, drug-abuse treatment, non-carceral rehabilitation, reparative justice, and restorative justice—could be developed and expanded now, notwithstanding the continued existence of prisons. With the widespread and effective use of these alternatives, many previously skeptical persons may come to trust them as crime-control strategies and thereby become more open to abandoning (or at least greatly limiting) the use of prisons. As Davis suggests, "The creation of new institutions that lay claim to the space now occupied by the prison can eventually start to crowd out the prison so that it would inhabit increasingly smaller areas of our social and psychic landscape."[8]

However, I am skeptical of three utopian elements in some strains of black radicalism. The first is the appeal to "radical imagination" when such appeals are unconstrained by what we know empirically or are not grounded in scientific knowledge. There is a tendency to call for the dismantling of long-standing practices (abolition) when we do not know what effects this would have or whether the predictable consequences would be tolerable or worth the effort. Here I believe it would benefit black critical theory to reduce (not abandon) its skepticism toward mainstream empirical social science, particularly quantitative and experimental studies of the effectiveness of law-enforcement efforts (see Chapter 5).

The second is the assumption, sometimes only implicit, that all wrongful aggression must be due either to structural injustice, imperialism, or mental illness. The optimistic thought seems to be that if we were to create just societies and a just global order, and to treat (rather than punish) those with mental illnesses, prisons would be obsolete. Yet interpersonal violence was prevalent before the emergence of racism and capitalism, even before Christian and Islamic imperialism, and in a wide variety of societies.[9] Another reason to suspect that there would be serious interpersonal wrongs even under just conditions is the existence of familiar human vices such as the thirst for power, greed, jealousy, lust, and wrath. These character flaws and temptations have been present in every society of recorded history, not just in capitalist or racist societies. And they are known to lead to great wrongdoing and social strife. These ordinary human failings are core themes of world literature going back centuries, and they are objects of long-standing religious prohibition in a range of faiths. It is therefore hard to believe that such vices would be eradicated by a just social order or by an end to class exploitation, empire, sexism, and racism.

And there is a third concern about some utopian thinking. The abolitionist project is a long-term one, requiring great changes not only in how we respond to harmful wrongdoing but also in how society is organized. And we don't really know how human beings would conduct themselves in the post-capitalist utopia. So, we shouldn't be so confident that prisons will not be needed. We also can't predict which technological innovations may occur in the future. These innovations could improve the practice of imprisonment (and policing), making it a more rehabilitative institution in addition to being safer and more humane; or, if we are lucky, maybe such innovations would make prisons obsolete.

Perhaps what we should say—and here I think this is also consistent with basic Marxist principles—is that we don't know enough about human nature to confidently predict what our dispositions and habits of mind would be under sociohistorical circumstances (including technological developments) that have never existed and that are radically different from the ones we now live under. But if that is so, we cannot say that we know that under fully just circumstances people without debilitating mental illness would not be inclined or tempted to engage in wrongful aggression against others. Although trying to create a society where prisons are not necessary is a laudable goal and a useful regulative ideal, we should be agnostic about whether prisons will be obsolete in a fully just society.

Systemic Injustice and
Structural Transformation

Radical abolitionists seek to dramatically alter U.S. society as a whole or perhaps even to transcend the global capitalist system. They maintain that these are deeply unjust social structures that require fundamental change. They recognize that our problems with racism, sexism, and xenophobia extend far beyond prisons and the police. It is somewhat puzzling, then, why abolitionists organize around dismantling prisons when their greater concern seems to be broader questions of social or global justice. Imprisonment is just one among a host of unjust practices within the basic structure of U.S. society and the global social order. Is there something special about imprisonment as a site of injustice that explains this theoretical and practical focus?

One hypothesis is that the prison system is a particularly egregious and salient example of these myriad forms of injustice. It serves as a microcosm of all that is wrong with existing social arrangements. Perhaps it is easier for people to accept that radical social change is necessary once they have understood and contemplated the many wrongs that the prison represents. If this is correct, I can see the wisdom of drawing people's attention to the prison problem insofar as it helps them better grasp the broader structural problem. This kind of theory and practice could function as political pedagogy, as a method of political education and a starting point for radical political engagement. What is still left unexplained, though, is why political resistance should be organized around abolishing prisons when it is the wider structural framework that needs to be changed.

Another hypothesis is that some abolitionists see prisons as a distinctive symptom of underlying structural injustice, a telling marker of an oppressive society.[10] Societies that make extensive use of prisons, their theory goes, do so to deal with injustices that would be handled better through a structural transformation of society itself. Of course, prisons exist in every country in the world, so the diagnosis would have to be that all existing societies are unjust, perhaps because of their reliance on capitalist practices and their endemic patriarchy and misogyny. But rather than elaborate a conception of social or global justice and defend it against rival visions, these abolitionists argue that we should change society and the world so that prisons are not needed. In a sense, that is their theory of justice: If we radically transform society so that it is unnecessary to impose incarceration to deal with social problems, justice would then (more or less) have been realized.

Yet this approach to critical theory and social change evades crucial and controversial questions of political morality. What are the principles of justice that we ought to realize, and which feasible forms of social life would satisfy these principles? If it turns out (as I think it does) that prisons are not inherently unjust and may be socially necessary even in a just social order, then the theory fails to identify what our most basic political aims ought to be. Prison abolition would then be an admirable but misdirected movement. Moreover, by using this approach—prison as reliable proxy for systemic injustice—we risk alienating potential allies in the struggle for structural transformation by creating polarizing disagreements over issues that are not fundamentally at stake. I will illustrate this point by returning to Davis.

Drawing inspiration from Du Bois's idea of "abolition democracy," Davis argues that social justice requires more than ending unjust practices. It must also include building new and more democratic institutions. In the case of unjust societies that rely heavily on prisons, she takes this argument a step further.[11] She argues that prisons are a reliable sign that fully democratic institutions have yet to be established. Part of imprisonment's function is to mitigate or contain the antisocial consequences of social problems—poverty, homelessness, inadequate education, drug abuse, lack of health care, and so on—that only a just social structure can truly solve. These social problems encourage criminal activity, which funnels the oppressed, neglected, and marginalized into prisons, only to release them even worse off. Those heavily burdened and marginalized by structural injustice cannot readily live crime-free lives without greater material resources, political empowerment, and basic social services. Deep structural and institutional reform of society would therefore, on Davis's account, make prisons unnecessary.

But this argument suggests that prisons are still necessary *now*, until such structural transformation has been brought about. Indeed, Davis says, "[Prisons] cannot, therefore, be eliminated unless new institutions and resources are made available to those communities that provide, in large part, the human beings that make up the prison population."[12] Prisons are not, then, obsolete. However, according to Davis, we should, through protracted and militant political struggle if necessary, do everything in our power to *make* them obsolete. We do this, in part, by creating genuinely democratic institutions that reject racism in all its forms and that show equal respect and concern for

everyone. These institutions should extend to political economy, which would mean not structuring social life around private wealth accumulation and the pursuit of profit.

However, if the existence of prisons is not a reliable sign of
structural injustice (because, say, imprisonment can be an effective and legitimate response to the problem of serious
crime), then the debate between prison reformers and abolitionists is a red herring and a distraction from what could be a
more basic common objective. I have argued that we have good
reasons to believe prisons can be reformed and not much reason to think we will ever fully transcend our need for prisons. I
strongly agree that there are far too many people in prison due
to structural injustice, but this does not mean that prisons
would be obsolete were justice realized. If I am right, it is the
existence of a vast prison population with a strikingly disproportionate representation of stigmatized and disadvantaged
social groups that is a sign of structural injustice. It is not the
existence of prisons per se.

Nevertheless, and this is the key point, both prison reformers
and abolitionists can, and should, share a goal: to fundamentally change the social conditions that so often give rise to the
need for punitive incarceration. Davis's four measures—greater
access to mental-health care, drug treatment, rehabilitation services, and mechanisms for transformative justice—are good
places to start. In societies like the United States, the kind of reform I favor would also include a restricted moratorium on the use
of prisons (which would be used to punish only the most serious
crimes) and on the use of certain policing tactics (those that
needlessly bring the police into close contact with black people),
joined with a commitment to broader structural reform.

The latter point is critical, because without a demonstrated commitment to structural reform from officials and from the public, imprisonment as a practice lacks legitimacy. The poor and racially stigmatized (who constitute most current and former prisoners in the United States) would have strong reasons to doubt that the criminal justice system serves to protect their interests even if due process procedures were scrupulously followed. If the structure of a society is deeply unjust, the oppressed will naturally conclude that penal policies are designed to protect the possessions and personal safety of the affluent and powerful at the expense of the disadvantaged and marginalized.

When I say that, upon reflection, I remain a reformer rather than an abolitionist, the scope of reform I imagine is not limited to prisons or policing or even to the criminal justice system more broadly. Like Davis, I think criminal justice reform is grossly inadequate unless it includes fighting for broader economic and racial justice. And such structural reform can also help to prevent crime.

For instance, the property-crime rate is *highly* sensitive to employment and wage rates.[13] Property crimes generally decline when employment and wages improve for low-skilled young men, and they rise when joblessness becomes more common and wages drop. Given the extreme wealth concentration, income inequality, and high rates of poverty that currently exist, corrective justice in the economic sphere is called for, independently of crime-control concerns. Many already have a legitimate claim on a fairer tax and subsidy scheme and on a job that pays a living wage or on a guaranteed basic income. Even setting aside these considerations of economic justice, if we want to prevent crime without relying primarily on prisons, then improving the economic circumstances of low-skilled young males would go a long way.

Rape, murder, and aggravated assault are much less responsive to labor market improvements, unfortunately. This is not surprising, given that such violence is often driven by motives other than money. Robbery, though a violent crime, is generally motivated by the prospects of material gain and so could be reduced by economic justice measures.

Prisons in the United States are disproportionately filled with black people, most of whom come from disadvantaged backgrounds or neighborhoods, and who have been convicted of property crimes, robbery, or drug offenses. As discussed in Chapter 3, extrinsic institutional racism in the criminal justice system reinforces stereotypes about black criminality, engenders fear of black males, and generally stigmatizes black people as deviant. These racial disparities in incarceration could be reduced through policy changes in law enforcement and sentencing. But we can also reduce them by preventing discrimination in the labor market and enhancing educational and economic opportunities for low-skilled black people.

There is no question that incarceration is grossly overused. It is sometimes dehumanizing; frequently abused; poorly administered; inadequately funded; and too closely tied to corporate profit. Far too often prisons are a vehicle for racial domination, economic exploitation, and political repression. Still, I am not convinced that abolishing prisons is morally required—or, at the moment, wise.

In the Unites States, grave background injustices (discrimination, failures in education, poverty, inequality, and so on) shape the ambitions and volition of some who commit crimes. Many are deeply disadvantaged by past or ongoing injustices, which can lead them to commit unlawful and sometimes violent acts—either out of need, frustration, despair, alienation, or defiance. To protect the vulnerable from wrongful aggression, it may be necessary to sentence the most violent of these oppressed offenders to prison.[14] This should be done reluctantly, with adequate support for reentry, and only after less harmful measures have been tried but failed.

What is most needed now is not so much to abolish prisons but to redress the systemic injustices that too often lead to crime and to the imprisonment of the oppressed. Or to put it in a slogan: Don't abolish the prison; abolish the ghetto.[15]

NOTES

Introduction. Reform or Abolition?

1. Emily Widra and Tiana Herring, "States of Incarceration: The Global Context," *Prison Policy Initiative*, September 2021.

2. LeRoy B. DePuy, "The Walnut Street Prison: Pennsylvania's First Penitentiary," *Pennsylvania History: A Journal of Mid-Atlantic Studies* 18 (1951): 130–144.

3. See, for example, Richard A. Viguerie, "A Conservative Case for Prison Reform," *New York Times*, June 9, 2013; David Dagan and Steven M. Teles, *Prison Break: Why Conservatives Turned against Mass Incarceration* (Oxford: Oxford University Press, 2016); and Arthur Rizer and Lars Trautman, "The Conservative Case for Criminal Justice Reform," *Guardian*, August 5, 2018.

4. For instance, Dylan Rodriguez says, "Reform is at best a form of casualty management, while reformism is counterinsurgency against those who dare to envision, enact, and experiment with abolitionist forms of community, collective power, and futurity. Abolition, in this sense, is the righteous nemesis of reformism, as well as the militant, principled, historically grounded response to liberal counterinsurgency." See Dylan Rodriguez, "Reformism Isn't Liberation, It's Counterinsurgency," *Level/Medium*, Oct. 20, 2020.

5. See Liat Ben-Moshe, "The Tension between Abolition and Reform," in *The End of Prisons: Reflections from the Decarceration Movement*, ed. Mechthild E. Nagel and Anthony J. Nocella II (n.p.: Brill, 2013), 83–92.

6. See, for example, Hugo Adam Bedau, *Killing as Punishment: Reflections on the Death Penalty in America* (Boston: Northeastern University, 2004); Carol S. Steiker, "No, Capital Punishment Is Not Morally Required: Deterrence, Deontology, and the Death Penalty," *Stanford Law Review* 58 (2005): 751–789; David Garland, *Peculiar Institution: America's Death Penalty in an Age of Abolition* (Oxford: Oxford University Press, 2010); Bryan Stevenson, *Just Mercy: A Story of Justice and Redemption* (New

York: Spiegel and Grau, 2014); and Michael Cholbi and Alex Madva, "Black Lives Matter and the Call for Death Penalty Abolition," *Ethics* 128 (2018): 517–544.

7. For an impressive attempt to draw together the vast and disparate writings of prison abolitionists into a coherent philosophy, starting with the 1998 Critical Resistance conference, see Dorothy E. Roberts, "Abolition Constitutionalism," *Harvard Law Review* 133, no. 1 (2019): 1–122. Yet even here, Roberts describes the movement's theory as "amorphous," and she focuses mainly on black radical and black feminist strands of thought, with much less attention to the pacifist and anarchist strands. A similar thing could be said about Julia C. Oparah, "Why No Prisons?" in *Why Prison?* ed. David Scott (Cambridge: Cambridge University Press, 2013).

8. Davis recounts her philosophical education and explains her conception of philosophy in *African-American Philosophers: 17 Conversations,* ed. George Yancy (New York: Routledge, 1998), 13–30.

9. Angela Y. Davis, *Abolition Democracy: Beyond Empire, Prisons, and Torture* (New York: Seven Stories Press, 2005), 23.

10. Davis, *Abolition Democracy,* 34.

11. Angela Y. Davis, *Are Prisons Obsolete?* (New York: Seven Stories Press, 2003).

12. Angela Y. Davis, *Freedom Is a Constant Struggle: Ferguson, Palestine, and the Foundations of a Movement* (Chicago: Haymarket Books, 2016), 7.

13. Angela Y. Davis, Gina Dent, Erica R. Meiners, and Beth E. Richie, *Abolition. Feminism. Now.* (Chicago: Haymarket Books, 2022), 42.

14. Davis, *Freedom Is a Constant Struggle,* 90.

15. In response to the question, "Is a prison- or jail-free society a utopia, or is it possible?" Davis has recently responded, "I do think that a society without prisons is a realistic future possibility, but in a transformed society, one in which people's needs, not profits, constitute the driving force." See Davis, *Freedom Is a Constant Struggle,* 6.

16. Cedric J. Robinson, *Black Marxism: The Making of the Black Radical Tradition* (Chapel Hill: University of North Carolina Press, 2000).

17. I situate my own approach to political philosophy in relation to the black radical tradition in "Afro-Analytical Marxism and the Problem of Race," in *The Proceedings and Addresses of the American Philosophical Association* 95 (November 2021): 37–60.

18. See John Rawls, *A Theory of Justice,* rev. ed. (Cambridge, MA: Belknap Press, 1999), xiv–xvi, 52–46, 239–251.

19. See Felicia R. Lee, "Academic Industrial Complex," *New York Times,* September 6, 2003.

20. My first attempt at this kind of synthesis is "Ideology, Racism, and Critical Social Theory," *Philosophical Forum* 34 (Summer 2003): 153–188.

21. Angela Y. Davis, "Afro Images: Politics, Fashion, and Nostalgia," in *The Angela Y. Davis Reader*, ed. Joy James (Malden, MA: Blackwell, 1998), 273–278.

22. See my *Dark Ghettos: Injustice, Dissent, and Reform* (Cambridge, MA: Belknap Press, 2016), chaps. 7–8.

23. For important work on the rise and problem of mass incarceration, see David Cole, *No Equal Justice: Race and Class in the American Criminal Justice System* (New York: New Press, 1999); Marc Mauer, *Race to Incarcerate* (New York: New Press, 1999); Bruce Western, *Punishment and Inequality in America* (New York: Russell Sage Foundation, 2006); Todd R. Clear, *Imprisoning Communities: How Mass Incarceration Makes Disadvantaged Neighborhoods Worse* (New York: Oxford University Press, 2007); Ruth Wilson Gilmore, *Golden Gulag: Prisons, Surplus, Crisis, and Opposition in Globalizing California* (Berkeley: University of California Press, 2007); Vesla M. Weaver, "Frontlash: Race and the Development of Punitive Crime Policy," *Studies in American Political Development* 21 (2007): 230–265; Glenn C. Loury, *Race, Incarceration, and American Values* (Cambridge, MA: MIT Press, 2008); Devah Pager, *Marked: Race, Crime, and Finding Work in an Era of Mass Incarceration* (Chicago: University of Chicago Press, 2008); Loïc Wacquant, *Punishing the Poor: The Neoliberal Government of Social Insecurity* (Durham, NC: Duke University Press, 2009); Michelle Alexander, *The New Jim Crow: Mass Incarceration in the Age of Colorblindness* (New York: New Press, 2010); Heather Ann Thompson, "Why Mass Incarceration Matters: Rethinking Crisis, Decline, and Transformation in Postwar American History," *Journal of American History* 97 (2010): 703–734; Marie Gottschalk, *Caught: The Prison State and the Lockdown of American Politics* (Princeton: Princeton University Press, 2014); Elizabeth Hinton, *From the War on Poverty to the War on Crime: The Making of Mass Incarceration in America* (Cambridge, MA: Harvard University Press, 2016); James Forman Jr., *Locking Up Our Own: Crime and Punishment in Black America* (New York: Farrar, Straus and Giroux, 2017); Kelly Lytle Hernández, *City of Inmates: Conquest, Rebellion, and the Rise of Human Caging in Los Angeles, 1771–1965* (Chapel Hill: UNC Press Books, 2017); John Pfaff, *Locked In: The True Causes of Mass Incarceration and How to Achieve Real Reform* (New York: Basic Books, 2017); and Bruce Western, *Homeward: Life in the Year After Prison* (New York: Russell Sage Foundation, 2018).

24. There are prominent prison reform organizations that are committed to broader social-structural reform, such as The Sentencing Project, the Equal Justice Initative, and the Vera Institute of Justice.

25. See, for example, Dan Berger, Mariame Kaba, and David Stein, "What Abolitionists Do," *Jacobin*, August 8, 2017.

Chapter 1. Political Prisoners and Black Radicalism

1. See, for example, Joy James, ed., *The New Abolitionists: (Neo)slave Narratives and Contemporary Prison Writings* (Albany: SUNY Press, 2005).

2. George Jackson, *Soledad Brother: The Prison Letters of George Jackson* (Chicago: Lawrence Hill Books, 1994), 68.

3. Jackson, *Soledad Brother*, 111.

4. Jackson, *Soledad Brother*, 7, 32.

5. Jackson, *Soledad Brother*, 106, 167–168.

6. Jackson, *Soledad Brother*, 118.

7. Huey P. Newton, *Revolutionary Suicide* (New York: Writers and Readers Publishing, 1995).

8. Newton, *Revolutionary Suicide*, 278–279.

9. Newton, *Revolutionary Suicide*, 197.

10. Assata Shakur, *Assata: An Autobiography* (London: Zed Books, 2016).

11. Shakur, *Assata*, 203.

12. Shakur, *Assata*, 52.

13. Shakur, *Assata*, 192.

14. Shakur, *Assata*, iiiv–ix.

15. Angela Davis, *Angela Davis: An Autobiography* (New York: International Publishers, 1974), 306.

16. Angela Y. Davis, ed., *If They Come in the Morning: Voices of Resistance* (New York: Verso Books, 2016), 39.

17. Shakur, *Assata*, 235.

18. Newton, *Revolutionary Suicide*, 184–186.

19. Davis, *Angela Davis*, 306.

20. Davis, *Angela Davis*, 317.

21. Davis, *If They Come in the Morning*, 23.

22. Davis, *Angela Davis*, 288.

23. Davis, *Angela Davis*, 312.

24. Davis, *Angela Davis*, 365.

25. Davis, *Angela Davis*, 23.

26. Jackson, *Soledad Brother*, 14.

27. Jackson, *Soledad Brother*, 25.

28. Davis, *If They Come in the Morning*, 29–30.

29. Davis, *If They Come in the Morning*, 33.

30. Davis, *If They Come in the Morning*, 62–63.

31. Newton, *Revolutionary Suicide*, 107.

32. Shakur, *Assata*, 60.

33. Shakur, *Assata*, 52.

34. Shakur, *Assata*, 65.

35. Shakur, *Assata*, 154.

36. For a defense of the need to abolish ghettos that draws on ideas from Huey Newton, see my *Dark Ghettos: Injustice, Dissent, and Reform* (Cambridge, MA: Harvard University Press, 2016).

37. See Davis, *Are Prisons Obsolete?*

38. Jackson, *Soledad Brother*, 4.

39. Shakur, *Assata*, 64.

40. Newton, *Revolutionary Suicide*, 282.

41. For a definitive account of the Attica uprising and the repressive response it engendered, see Heather Ann Thompson, *Blood in the Water: The Attica Prison Uprising of 1971 and Its Legacy* (New York: Vintage, 2017).

42. Davis, *If They Come in the Morning*, 46.

43. Davis, *If They Come in the Morning*, 40.

Chapter 2. Punishment, Dehumanization, and Slavery

1. Malcolm X and Alex Haley, *The Autobiography of Malcolm X* (New York: Random House,1965), 176.

2. "Prisons: The Siege of Cherry Hill," *Time*, January 31, 1955.

3. Malcolm X and Alex Haley, *Autobiography of Malcolm X*, 181.

4. Abolitionists frequently describe incarcerated persons as being in "cages." Yet the small-occupancy, locked-in cell (1–2 persons), though often used, is not essential to incarceration. Some prisons (for example, many minimum-to-low-security prisons) are internally organized with prisoners quartered in large rooms with many occupants, in cubicle quarters, or in open dormitories. Small cells for one or two occupants are most common in medium-to-maximum-security prisons, where prisoners have committed violent offenses or have a history of violence toward other prisoners or prison staff. Where higher levels of security are necessary, the cell does, however, lessen the need for supervisory personnel and so may save money. It can also reduce the need for constant surveillance (to prevent harm or escape) and so could (at least when limited to one occupant) also provide some privacy for prisoners.

5. Davis, *Are Prisons Obsolete?*, 41.

6. See, for example, Jenna M. Loyd, Matt Mitchelson, and Andrew Burridge, ed., *Beyond Walls and Cages: Prisons, Borders, and Global Crisis* (Athens: University of Georgia Press, 2012).

7. For helpful discussions of the issue, see Joseph H. Carens, *The Ethics of Immigration* (Oxford: Oxford University Press, 2013); Michael Blake, "Immigration, Jurisdiction, and Exclusion," *Philosophy & Public Affairs* 41 (2013): 103–130; José Jorge Mendoza, *The Moral and Political Philosophy of Immigration: Liberty, Security, and Equality* (Lexington Books, 2016); Christopher Bertram, *Do States Have the Right to Exclude Immigrants* (Cambridge: Polity, 2018); Anna Stilz, *Territorial Sovereignty: A Philosophical Exploration* (Oxford: Oxford University Press, 2019); Adam Hosein, *The Ethics of Migration: An Introduction* (Routledge, 2019).

8. Angela Y. Davis, *The Meaning of Freedom* (San Francisco: City Lights Books, 2012), 59.

9. Davis, *Are Prisons Obsolete?*, 44.

10. See Danielle Allen, "Imprisonment in Classical Athens," *Classical Quarterly* 47 (1997): 121–135.

11. See Judith Resnik, "(Un)Constitutional Punishments: Eighth Amendment Silos, Penological Purposes, and People's 'Ruin,'" *Yale Law Journal Forum* 129 (2019): 365–415; Justin Driver and Emma Kaufman, "The Incoherence of Prison Law," *Harvard Law Review* 135 (2021): 515–584.

12. Some contemporary philosophical writings on punishment that I have found especially illuminating include John Rawls, "Two Concepts of Rules" *Philosophical Review* 64 (1955): 3–32; S. I. Benn, "An Approach to the Problems of Punishment," *Philosophy* 33 (1958): 325–341; Joel Feinberg, "The Expressive Function of Punishment," *The Monist* 49 (1965): 397–423; H.L.A. Hart, "Prolegomena to the Principles of Punishment," in *Punishment and Responsibility: Essays in the Philosophy of Law* (Oxford: Oxford University Press, 1968), 1–27; Herbert Morris, "Persons and Punishment," *Monist* 52 (1968): 475–501; Jeffrie G. Murphy, "Marxism and Retribution," *Philosophy and Public Affairs* 2 (1973): 217–243; Richard W. Burgh, "Do the Guilty Deserve Punishment?," *Journal of Philosophy* 79 (1982): 193–210; Jean Hampton, "The Moral Education Theory of Punishment," *Philosophy and Public Affairs* 13 (1984): 208–238; Warren Quinn, "The Right to Threaten and the Right to Punish," *Philosophy and Public Affairs* 14 (1985): 327–373; Daniel M. Farrell, "The Justification of General Deterrence," *Philosophical Review* 94 (1985): 367–394; George Sher, *Desert* (Princeton: Princeton University Press, 1987), chap. 5; Uma Narayan, "Appropriate Responses and Preventive Benefits: Justifying Censure and Hard Treatment," *Oxford Journal of Legal Studies* 13 (1993): 166–182; R. A. Duff, *Punishment, Communication,*

and Community (Oxford: Oxford University Press, 2001); T. M. Scanlon, "Punishment and the Rule of Law," in *The Difficulty of Tolerance: Essays in Political Philosophy* (New York: Cambridge University Press, 2003), 219–233; Victor Tadros, *The Ends of Harm: The Moral Foundations of Criminal Law* (Oxford: Oxford University Press, 2011); Christopher Heath Wellman, "The Rights Forfeiture Theory of Punishment." *Ethics* 122 (2012): 371–393; Erin I. Kelly, *The Limits of Blame: Rethinking Punishment and Responsibility* (Cambridge, MA: Harvard University Press, 2018).

13. Davis, *Freedom Is a Constant Struggle*, 22.

14. Some who are sympathetic to abolition argue for a dramatic increase in electronic monitoring and surveillance and a corresponding decrease in imprisonment. See, for example, Mirko Bargaric, Dan Hunter, and Jennifer Svilar, "Prison Abolition: From Naïve Idealism to Technological Pragmatism," *Journal of Criminal Law and Criminology* 111 (2021): 351–406. However, others regard such measures as the functional equivalent of prison and reject them on similar grounds. See, for example, Maya Schenwar and Victoria Law, *Prison By Any Other Name: The Harmful Consequences of Popular Reforms* (New York: The New Press, 2020). For reasons to not penalize property crimes with imprisonment, see Andrew Ashworth, "What If Imprisonment Were Abolished for Property Offenses?," The Howard League for Penal Reform, 2013.

15. See, for example, James Q. Whitman, *Harsh Justice: Criminal Punishment and the Widening Divide between America and Europe* (Oxford University Press, 2004); Ram Subramanian and Alison Shames, "Sentencing and Prison Practices in Germany and the Netherlands: Implications for the United States," Center on Sentencing and Corrections (New York: Vera Institute of Justice, 2013); Marc Morjé Howard, *Unusually Cruel: Prisons, Punishment, and the Real American Exceptionalism* (Oxford University Press, 2017); David Skarbek, *The Puzzle of Order: Why Life Behind Bars Varies around the World* (Oxford University Press, 2020).

16. See "Supermax: A Curated Collection of Links," *The Marshall Project*, December 29, 2019, https://www.themarshallproject.org/records/3388-supermax.

17. Craig Haney, "Mental Health Issues in Long-term Solitary and 'Supermax' Confinement," *Crime and Delinquency* 49 (2003): 124–156; Stuart Grassian, "Psychiatric Effects of Solitary Confinement," *Washington University Journal of Law and Policy* 22 (2006): 325–383.

18. I attempt to satisfy this burden in *Dark Ghettos: Injustice, Dissent, and Reform* (Cambridge, MA: Belknap Press, 2016), chap. 8.

19. Prisoners are deprived of some ordinary rights to protect prisoners and prison staff and to prevent escape. Custodial care and the imposition of sentences require

these interferences with prisoners' freedom. But perhaps beyond these, prisoners should retain their full rights where feasible. One issue is that many rights prisoners might like to claim (and whose exercise wouldn't interfere with the imposition of their sentence) would cost the public to facilitate (for example, communications with the outside world through mail delivery, internet service, or phone service). Most of these costs the public can be expected to absorb, as they are not high or are made artificially high due to monopoly. There is, however, a question of how far the public should be expected to go in facilitating the exercise of prisoner's rights. There is also a question of whether prisoners can be expected to help cover these costs.

20. I should note that there are some radical abolitionists who believe that we should never resort to the practice of psychiatric incarceration, not even for suicidal adolescents or for mentally ill persons who pose a grave danger to others. Here, confinement and segregation are regarded as components of a "carceral logic" that must always be opposed and that no cost-benefit analysis could ever justify. See, for example, Liat Ben-Moshe, *Decarcerating Disability: Deinstitutionalization and Prison Abolition* (University of Minnesota Press, 2020).

21. Davis, *Freedom Is a Constant Struggle*, 138.

22. See, for example, Steve Martinot, "Toward the Abolition of the Prison System," *Socialism and Democracy* 28 (2014): 189–198.

23. See Angela Y. Davis, Gina Dent, Erica R. Meiners, and Beth E. Richie, *Abolition. Feminism. Now.* (Chicago: Haymarket Books, 2022).

24. See Ashley Farmer, "Free Joan Little: Anti-rape Activism, Black Power, and the Black Freedom Movement," *Black Perspectives*, February 4, 2016. Also see Mariame Kaba, "'Free Joan Little': Reflections on Prisoner Resistance and Movement Building," *Prison Culture*, June 4, 2011.

25. Angela Davis, "Joan Little: The Dialectics of Rape," *Ms. Magazine*, June 1975.

26. Anarchism comes in many varieties and is an old political philosophy, often associated with thinkers such as Pierre-Joseph Proudhon, Mikhail Bakunin, Peter Kropotkin, and William Godwin. Influential contemporary defenses of philosophical anarchism include Robert Paul Wolff, *In Defense of Anarchism* (New York: Harper & Row, 1970); A. John Simmons, *On the Edge of Anarchy* (Princeton: Princeton University Press, 1993). For a defense of anarchism in the black radical tradition, see Lorenzo Kom'boa Ervin, *Anarchism and the Black Revolution: The Definitive Edition* (London: Pluto Press, 2021).

27. For a classic statement and defense of this position, see Emma Goldman, "Anarchism: What It Really Stands For" and "Prisons: A Social Crime and Failure," both in *Anarchism and Other Essays* (New York: Dover Publications, 1969), 47–68, 109–126.

The view is also defended within the black radical tradition in, for example, William C. Anderson, *The Nation on No Map: Black Anarchism and Abolition* (Edinburgh: AK Press, 2021).

28. Davis, *Abolition Democracy*, 34.

29. Davis, *Abolition Democracy*, 35; Davis, *Freedom Is a Constant Struggle*, 88. Also see Brady Thomas Heiner, "From the Prison of Slavery to the Slavery of Prison." *Radical Philosophy Today* 5 (2007): 219–227.

30. Davis, *Abolition Democracy*, 73–74.

31. Davis, *The Meaning of Freedom*, 52.

32. Angela Y. Davis, "From the Prison of Slavery to the Slavery of Prison: Frederick Douglass and the Convict Lease System," in *The Angela Y. Davis Reader*, ed. Joy James (Malden: Blackwell, 1998), 74–95.

33. See C.L.R. James, *Black Jacobins: Toussaint L'Ouverture and the Santa Domingo Revolution* (New York: Vintage Books, 1989).

34. See, for example, Angela Y. Davis, "Reflections on the Black Women's Role in the Community of Slaves," in *The Angela Y. Davis Reader*, ed. Joy James (Malden: Blackwell, 1998), 111–128.

35. David M. Perry, "Our Long, Troubling History of Sterilizing the Incarcerated," The Marshall Project, July 26, 2017, https://www.themarshallproject.org/2017/07/26/our-long-troubling-history-of-sterilizing-the-incarcerated.

36. See Stuart White, *The Civic Minimum: On the Rights and Obligations of Economic Citizenship* (Oxford University Press, 2003); and Lucas Stanczyk, "Productive Justice," *Philosophy & Public Affairs* 40, no. 2 (2012): 144–164.

37. Paying prisoners below a market wage might drive down wages for those not incarcerated, so that might be a reason to pay market wages. However, the wrong of not doing so, if it's a wrong, would not be a wrong to prisoners. For a historical perspective on this long-standing issue, see Rebecca M. McLennan, *The Crisis of Imprisonment: Protest, Politics, and the Making of the American Penal State, 1776–1941* (Cambridge: Cambridge University Press, 2008).

38. Some of the revenue from prison labor could also be used to compensate victims or their families for harm they have suffered.

39. You can see the Prison Policy Initiative figures in Wendy Sawyer, "How Much Do Incarcerated People Earn in Each State?" Prison Policy Initiative, April 10, 2017, https://www.prisonpolicy.org/blog/2017/04/10/wages/.

40. For useful discussions of this issue, see Rex Martin, *A System of Rights* (Oxford: Clarendon Press, 1993), chap. 11; and Richard L. Lippke, "Prison Labor: Its Control, Facilitation, and Terms," *Law and Philosophy* 17 (1998): 533–557.

41. See Raymond Geuss, "Genealogy as Critique," *European Journal of Philosophy* 10 (2002): 209–215; David Owen, "Criticism and Captivity: On Genealogy and Critical Theory," *European Journal of Philosophy* 10 (2002): 216–230.

42. See Davis, *Are Prisons Obsolete?*, 77; Davis, "From the Prison of Slavery to the Slavery of Prison," 76; Davis, *The Meaning of Freedom*, 52, 127, 137.

43. Davis, *The Meaning of Freedom*, 52.

44. Bruce Western, *Punishment and Inequality in America* (New York: Russell Sage Foundation, 2006).

45. Robert T. Chase, *We Are Not Slaves: State Violence, Coerced Labor, and Prisoners' Rights in Postwar America* (Chapel Hill: University of North Carolina Press, 2019).

Chapter 3. Racism and Functional Critique

1. Angela Y. Davis, *The Meaning of Freedom* (San Francisco: City Lights Books, 2012), 47–49.

2. Angela Y. Davis, "Racialized Punishment and Prison Abolition," in *The Angela Y. Davis Reader*, ed. Joy James (Malden: Blackwell, 1998), 105.

3. Davis, *The Meaning of Freedom*, 37.

4. Angela Y. Davis, *Freedom Is a Constant Struggle: Ferguson, Palestine, and the Foundations of a Movement* (Chicago: Haymarket Books, 2016), 24–25.

5. There is an important debate over the validity and centrality of functional explanation in Marxist social theory. For example, G. A. Cohen has argued that the central claims of historical materialism (Marx's theory of history) are not coherent or plausible unless functional explanation is a valid form of scientific explanation. I will not weigh in on this debate but will assume that at least some forms of functional explanation are valid. For details, see G. A. Cohen, *Karl Marx's Theory of History: A Defense*, Expanded Edition (Princeton: Princeton University Press, 2000), chaps. 9–10. For criticisms of functional explanation in the context of Marxist theory, see Jon Elster, "Marxism, Functionalism, and Game Theory," in *Debates In Contemporary Political Philosophy: An Anthology*, ed. Derek Matravers and Jon Pike (London: Routledge, 1990), 22–40.

6. For instance, influential abolitionist organizer Mariame Kaba says: "Importantly, we must reject all talk about policing and the overall criminal punishment system being 'broken' or 'not working.' By rhetorically constructing the criminal punishment system as 'broken,' reform is reaffirmed and abolition is painted as unrealistic and unworkable." Mariame Kaba, *We Do This 'Til We Free Us: Abolitionist Organizing and Transforming Justice* (Chicago: Haymarket Books, 2021), 49.

7. Robert K. Merton, *Social Theory and Social Structure* (New York: Free Press, 1968), 104–105.

8. Davis, "Racialized Punishment and Prison Abolition," 102–105. Also see Davis, *The Meaning of Freedom*, chap. 3.

9. Angela Y. Davis, *Are Prisons Obsolete?* (New York: Seven Stories Press, 2003), 25.

10. See Patrisse Cullors, "Abolition and Reparations: Histories of Resistance, Transformative Justice, and Accountability," *Harvard Law Review* 132 (2019): 1684–1694; Colin Kaepernick, "The Demand for Abolition," *Level/Medium*, October 6, 2020.

11. Davis, *The Meaning of Freedom*, 30.

12. Davis, *The Meaning of Freedom*, 38–40; Angela Y. Davis, From the Prison of Slavery to the Slavery of Prison: Frederick Douglass and the Convict Lease System," in *The Angela Y. Davis Reader*, ed. Joy James (Malden: Blackwell, 1998), 74–95.

13. Davis, *The Meaning of Freedom*, 117.

14. Davis, *The Meaning of Freedom*, 124.

15. Angela Y. Davis, "Race and Criminalization: Black Americans and the Punishment Industry," in *The Angela Y. Davis Reader*, 66–67. Also see Khalil Gibran Muhammad, *The Condemnation of Blackness: Race, Crime, and the Making of Modern Urban America* (Cambridge, MA: Harvard University Press, 2010); and Elizabeth Hinton and DeAnza Cook, "The Mass Criminalization of Black Americans: A Historical Overview," *Annual Review of Criminology* 4 (2021): 261–286.

16. Davis, "From the Prison of Slavery to the Slavery of Prison," 91–92. Also see Davis, *The Meaning of Freedom*, 38–39.

17. George M. Fredrickson, *Racism: A Short History* (Princeton: Princeton University Press, 2002); Ibram X. Kendi, *Stamped from the Beginning: The Definitive History of Racist Ideas in America* (New York: Random House, 2017).

18. Derrick Darby and John L. Rury, *The Color of Mind: Why the Origins of the Achievement Gap Matter for Justice* (Chicago: University of Chicago Press, 2018).

19. Davis, *Are Prisons Obsolete?*, 85–86.

20. As David Garland says, "American penality is often referred to today as "mass incarceration" as if there were a singular project or characteristic to which penal policy might be reduced. But America's local, state, and federal penal systems are complex assemblages of laws, policies, and practices, which have emerged and evolved over time. Far from being the realization of some national plan, what we call "mass incarceration" is the cumulative result of multiple contributing causes, operating at distinct governmental levels, prompted by different events and considerations, involving diverse political actors and coalitions, and enacted in thousands of laws, policies, and enforcement practices." David Garland, "Penal Controls and

Social Controls: Toward a Theory of American Penal Exceptionalism," *Punishment and Society* 22 (2020): 327.

21. Angela Y. Davis, "Political Prisoners, Prisons, and Black Liberation," in *The Angela Y. Davis Reader*, 44.

22. Davis, "Political Prisoners, Prisons, and Black Liberation," 45.

23. Davis, "Race and Criminalization," 67.

24. Davis, "Race and Criminalization," 64–66.

25. See, for example, Thomas Mathiesen, "The Politics of Abolition," *Contemporary Crises* 10 (1986): 81–94.

26. The classic statement is found in Kwame Ture (Stokely Carmichael) and Charles V. Hamilton, *Black Power: The Politics of Liberation in America* (New York: Vintage, 1992).

Chapter 4. The Prison Industrial Complex

1. Davis, *Are Prisons Obsolete?*, ch. 5; Davis, *The Meaning of Freedom*, ch. 2; Davis, *Freedom Is a Constant Struggle*, ch. 4.

2. Davis, *Are Prisons Obsolete?*, 12, 86–88; Davis, *The Meaning of Freedom*, 54–55. Also see Ruth Wilson Gilmore, "Abolition Geography and the Problem of Innocence," *Tabula Rasa* 28 (2018): 57–77.

3. Angela Y. Davis, "Masked Racism: Reflections on the Prison Industrial Complex," *Colorlines*, September 10, 1998.

4. Davis, *Freedom Is a Constant Struggle*, 5–6.

5. Davis, *Freedom Is a Constant Struggle*, 65, 107.

6. Davis, *Are Prisons Obsolete?*, 36–37. Also see Davis, *Freedom Is a Constant Struggle*, 24.

7. See Ruth Wilson Gilmore, *Golden Gulag: Prisons, Surplus, Crisis, and Opposition in Globalizing California* (University of California Press, 2007).

8. Davis, *Are Prisons Obsolete?*, 90–91, 98–100.

9. For a defense of the nonprofit alternative, with a focus on its possible contribution to prisoner rehabilitation, see Daniel L. Low, "Nonprofit Private Prisons: The Next Generation of Prison Management," *New England Journal on Criminal and Civil Confinement* 29 (2003): 1. Also see Richard Moran, "A Third Option: Nonprofit Prisons," *New York Times*, August 23, 1997; and David Pozen, "The Private, Nonprofit Prison," *Boston Globe*, February 21, 2006.

10. This already occurs with some juvenile corrections institutions, and there is some evidence that the practice could be extended to adult prisons with beneficial

consequences for recidivism. See Patrick Bayer and David E. Pozen, "The Effectiveness of Juvenile Correctional Facilities: Public versus Private Management," *Journal of Law and Economics* 48, no. 2 (2005): 549–589; and Mattheus Wassenaar, Raymond Gradus, and Toon Molleman, "Are Nonprofit Prisons an Alternative? Some Experiences in the Netherlands," *Nonprofit Management and Leadership* 28 (2018): 529–537.

11. Compare Avihay Dorfman and Alon Harel, "The Case against Privatization," *Philosophy and Public Affairs* 41.1 (2013): 67–102. Also see Chiara Cordelli, "Privatization without Profit," in *Privatization: NOMOS LX* (New York: NYU Press, 2018).

12. For details, see James Queally, "What Happened to Sandra Bland before She Died in a Texas Jail?" *Los Angeles Times*, July 28, 2015; Clifford Ward, "Failure to be Bonded Out Led Sandra Bland to Suicide, Officials Allege," *Chicago Tribune*, November 12, 2015; Adeel Hassan, "The Sandra Bland Video: What We Know," *New York Times*, May 7, 2019; and David Montgomery, "The Death of Sandra Bland: Is There Anything Left to Investigate?" *New York Times*, May 8, 2019.

Chapter 5. Incarceration and Its Alternatives

1. Steven N. Durlauf, "The Deterrent Effect of Imprisonment," in *Controlling Crime: Strategies and Tradeoffs*, ed. Daniel S. Nagin (Chicago: University of Chicago Press, 2012), 44–93; Daniel S. Nagin, "Deterrence in the Twenty-First Century," *Crime and Justice* 42 (2013): 199–263; David Roodman, "The Impacts of Incarceration on Crime," available at Social Science Research Network 3635864 (2017); Sarah Tahamont and Aaron Chalfin, "The Effect of Prisons on Crime," in *The Oxford Handbook of Prisons and Imprisonment*, ed. John Wooldredge and Paula Smith (Oxford: Oxford University Press, 2018), 628–651.

2. See Rucker Johnson and Steven Raphael, "How Much Crime Reduction Does the Marginal Prisoner Buy?" *Journal of Law and Economics* 55 (2012): 275–310; Raymond V. Liedka, Anne Morrison Piehl, and Bert Useem, "The Crime-Control Effect of Incarceration: Does Scale Matter?" *Criminology and Public Policy* 5, no. 2 (2006): 245–276.

3. See Weihua Li, David Eads, and Jamiles Lartey, "There Are Fewer People behind Bars Now Than 10 Years Ago. Will It Last?" *The Marshall Project*, September 20, 2021, https://www.themarshallproject.org/2021/09/20/there-are-fewer-people-behind-bars-now-than-10-years-ago-will-it-last; and Sintia Radu, "Countries with the Highest Incarceration Rates," *U.S. News & World Report*, May 13, 2019.

4. See Mark A. R. Kleiman, *When Brute Force Fails: How to Have Less Crime and Less Punishment* (Princeton: Princeton University Press, 2009).

5. Daniel S. Nagin, "Deterrence: A Review of the Evidence by a Criminologist for Economists," *Annual Review of Economics* 5 (2013), 89. Also see Steven N. Durlauf and Daniel S. Nagin, "Imprisonment and Crime: Can Both Be Reduced?" *Criminology and Public Policy* 10 (2011): 13–54; Steven D. Levitt, "Understanding Why Crime Fell in the 1990s: Four Factors That Explain the Decline and Six That Do Not," *Journal of Economic Perspectives* 18, no. 1(2004): 163–190; Raymond Paternoster, "How Much Do We Really Know about Criminal Deterrence?" *Journal of Criminal Law and Criminology* 100 (2010): 765–824.

6. Aaron Chalfin and Justin McCrary, "Criminal Deterrence: A Review of the Literature," *Journal of Economic Literature* 55 (2017): 5–48; National Academies of Sciences, Engineering, and Medicine, *Proactive Policing: Effects on Crime and Communities* (Washington, DC: The National Academies Press, 2018); Patrick Sharkey, *Uneasy Peace: The Great Crime Decline, the Renewal of City Life, and the Next War on Violence* (W. W. Norton & Company, 2018), chap. 3; Anthony A. Braga, Brandon Turchan, Andrew V. Papachristos, and David M. Hureau, "Hot Spots Policing of Small Geographic Areas Effects on Crime," *Campbell Systematic Reviews* (2019): 1–88; Daniel S. Nagin and Robert J. Sampson, "The Real Gold Standard: Measuring Counterfactual Worlds That Matter to Social Science and Policy," *Annual Review of Criminology* 2 (2019): 123–45.

7. See Braga et al., "Hot Spots Policing."

8. See Jennifer L. Eberhardt, Phillip Atiba Goff, Valerie J. Purdie, and Paul G. Davies, "Seeing Black: Race, Crime, and Visual Processing," *Journal of Personality and Social Psychology* 87, no. 6 (2004): 876–893; Paul Butler, *Chokehold: Policing Black Men* (New York: New Press, 2017); Tracey L. Meares, "Policing: A Public Good Gone Bad," *Boston Review*, August 1, 2017; Joe Soss and Vesla Weaver, "Police Are Our Government: Politics, Political Science, and the Policing of Race–Class Subjugated Communities," *Annual Review of Political Science* 20 (2017): 565–591; and Elizabeth Hinton, *America on Fire: The Untold History of Police Violence and Black Rebellion Since the 1960s* (New York: Liveright Publishing, 2021).

9. Robert J. Sampson and Dawn Jeglum Bartusch, "Legal Cynicism and (Subcultural?) Tolerance of Deviance: The Neighborhood Context of Racial Differences," *Law and Society Review* 32 (1998): 777–804; Rick Trinkner and Phillip Atiba Goff, "The Color of Safety: The Psychology of Race and Policing," in *The SAGE Handbook of Global Policing*, ed. Ben Bradford, Beatrice Jauregui, Ian Loader, and Jonny Steinberg (London: Sage Publications, 2016): 61–81; Monica C. Bell, "Police Reform and the Dismantling of Legal Estrangement," *Yale Law Journal* 126 (2017): 2054–2150.

10. Tracey Meares, "Broken Windows, Neighborhoods, and the Legitimacy of Law Enforcement or Why I Fell in and out of Love with Zimbardo," *Journal of*

Research in Crime and Delinquency 52 (2015): 609–625. Also see Tom R. Tyler, *Why People Obey the Law* (New Haven: Yale University Press, 1990).

11. See, for example, Derecka Purnell, *Becoming Abolitionists: Police, Protest, and the Pursuit of Freedom* (New York: Verso Books, 2021); Mariame Kaba, *We Do This 'Til We Free Us: Abolitionist Organizing and Transforming Justice* (Chicago: Haymarket Books, 2021); Rinaldo Walcott, *On Property: Policing, Prisons, and the Call for Abolition* (Windsor, Ontario: Biblioasis, 2021); Micol Seigel, *Violence Work: State Power and the Limits of Police* (Durham, NC: Duke University Press, 2018); and Alex S. Vitale, *The End of Policing* (New York: Verso Books, 2017).

12. Adam Omar Hosein, "Racial Profiling and the Reasonable Sense of Inferior Political Status," *Journal of Political Philosophy* 26 (2018): e1–e20.

13. Daniel S. Nagin, Francis T. Cullen, and Cheryl Lero Jonson, "Imprisonment and Reoffending," *Crime and Justice* 38 (2009): 115–200.

14. See Devah Pager, *Marked: Race, Crime, and Finding Work in an Era of Mass Incarceration* (Chicago: University of Chicago Press, 2007); Christopher Uggen, Jeff Manza, and Melissa Thompson, "Citizenship, Democracy, and the Civic Reintegration of Criminal Offenders," *The Annals of the American Academy of Political and Social Science* 605, no. 1 (2006): 281–310; Michelle Alexander, *The New Jim Crow: Mass Incarceration in the Age of Colorblindness* (New York: The New Press, 2010).

15. See, for example, James Q. Whitman, *Harsh Justice: Criminal Punishment and the Widening Divide between America and Europe* (Oxford: Oxford University Press, 2004); Ram Subramanian and Alison Shames, "Sentencing and Prison Practices in Germany and the Netherlands: Implications for the United States," Center on Sentencing and Corrections (New York: Vera Institute of Justice, 2013); Marc Morjé Howard, *Unusually Cruel: Prisons, Punishment, and the Real American Exceptionalism* (New York: Oxford University Press, 2017); David Skarbek, *The Puzzle of Order: Why Life Behind Bars Varies around the World* (Oxford: Oxford University Press, 2020).

16. Jeffrey Fagan and Tracey L. Meares, "Punishment, Deterrence and Social Control: The Paradox of Punishment in Minority Communities," *Ohio State Journal of Criminal Law* 6 (2008): 173–230.

17. For a helpful and insightful discussion of this and related issues, see Christopher Lewis, "Inequality, Incentives, Criminality, and Blame," *Legal Theory* 22 (2016): 153–180.

18. Davis, *Are Prisons Obsolete?*, 108–110.

19. Davis, *The Meaning of Freedom*, 39.

20. Davis, *Freedom Is a Constant Struggle*, 22.

21. Davis, *The Meaning of Freedom*, 143.

22. All else being equal, a society without prisons would be better—more humane and decent—than one that uses them. But what if relying solely on prison alternatives to deal with violent crime would cost the public a lot, say, two or three times as much? For example, home confinement and electronic monitoring with ample law enforcement nearby to prevent unauthorized movement might be effective but financially costly. Could a society still be just (though not perfectly good) if it chose to rely on prisons rather than pay these higher costs? I'm not sure how to answer this question, but I think it's worth asking.

23. See Patrisse Cullors, "Abolition and Reparations: Histories of Resistance, Transformative Justice, and Accountability," *Harvard Law Review* 132 (2018): 1684–1694; Allegra M. McLeod, "Envisioning Abolition Democracy," *Harvard Law Review* 132 (2019): 1613–1649; Beth E. Richie and Kayla M. Martensen, "Resisting Carcerality, Embracing Abolition: Implications for Feminist Social Work Practice," *Affilia: Journal of Women and Social Work* 35 (2020): 12–16; Mariame Kaba, *We Do This 'Til We Free Us*; Mimi E. Kim, "Transformative Justice and Restorative Justice: Gender-Based Violence and Alternative Visions of Justice in the United States," *International Review of Victimology* (2021): 162–172; Amanda Alexander and Danielle Sered, "Making Communities Safe, without the Police," *Boston Review,* November 1, 2021; Angela Y. Davis, Gina Dent, Erica R. Meiners, and Beth E. Richie, *Abolition. Feminism. Now.* (Chicago: Haymarket Books, 2022).

24. Davis, *Are Prisons Obsolete?*, 114–115.

25. Kimbriell Kelly, "In a Home Surrounded by Homicide," *Washington Post,* November 16, 2018.

26. Heather Nolan, "Man Pleads Guilty in 2014 Algiers Homicide, Attempted Homicide of Victim's Cousin," *The Times-Picayune,* March 19, 2019.

Chapter 6. Utopian Imagination and Structural Transformation

1. For an influential discussion of these concerns, see Charles W. Mills, "'Ideal Theory' as Ideology," *Hypatia* 20, no. 3 (2005): 165–183.

2. Tommie Shelby, "Racial Realities and Corrective Justice: A Reply to Charles Mills," *Critical Philosophy of Race* 1, no. 2 (2013): 145–162.

3. Karl Marx, *Capital: A Critique of Political Economy,* vol. 1, trans. Ben Fowkes (New York: Vintage, 1977), 899.

4. Davis, *Are Prisons Obsolete?*, 20–21. Also see Davis, *The Meaning of Freedom,* 82; and Davis, *Freedom Is a Constant Struggle,* 100.

5. A view along these lines is developed in Allegra M. McLeod, "Prison Abolition and Grounded Justice." *UCLA Law Review* 62 (2015): 1156–1239.

6. See Robin D. G. Kelley, *Freedom Dreams: The Black Radical Imagination* (Boston: Beacon Press, 2002).

7. See Allegra M. McLeod, "Envisioning Abolition Democracy," *Harvard Law Review* 132 (2019): 1613–1649.

8. Davis, *Are Prisons Obsolete?*, 107–108.

9. Debra L. Martin and David W. Frayer, ed., *Troubled Times: Violence and Warfare in the Past* (London: Routledge, 1997); Phillip L. Walker "A Bioarchaeological Perspective on the History of Violence," *Annual Review of Anthropology* 30 (2001): 573–596.

10. For instance, well-known and influential abolitionist Ruth Wilson Gilmore says, "Worldwide today, wherever inequality is deepest, the use of prison as a catchall solution to social problems prevails—nowhere as extensively as in the United States, led by California." See Ruth Wilson Gilmore, "Abolition Geography and the Problem of Innocence," *Tabula Rasa* 28 (2018): 57–77.

11. Angela Y. Davis, *Abolition Democracy: Beyond Empire, Prisons, and Torture* (New York: Seven Stories Press, 2005), 96–97, 118–119.

12. Davis, *Abolition Democracy*, 96–97.

13. Eric D. Gould, Bruce A. Weinberg, and David B. Mustard, "Crime Rates and Local Labor Market Opportunities in the United States: 1979–1997," *Review of Economics and Statistics* 84 (2002): 45–61.

14. See my *Dark Ghettos: Injustice, Dissent, and Reform* (Cambridge, MA: Belknap Press, 2016), chap. 8.

15. I thank Christopher Lewis for suggesting this slogan.

INDEX

abolition feminism, 7, 64, 174
abolitionism/anti-slavery movement,
    20, 21, 45
abolitionist theory. *See* prison abolition
abstraction, in philosophical argument,
    184–86
academic industrial complex, 13
Adorno, Theodor W., 9
Afro-analytical Marxism, 14
agency, 59–63
Alligood, Clarence, 64
alternatives to prison, 149–71; commu-
    nity accountability, 171–72; compat-
    ible with use of incarceration, 166;
    costs of, 218n22; Davis on, 166, 192,
    198; deterrence and, 150–62; evalua-
    tion of, 153; mental-health care,
    167–68; moratorium on imprison-
    ment and, 115, 116; preferability of,
    53, 119, 123, 149, 171; rehabilitation,
    169–70; substance use and addiction
    treatment, 168–69; transformative
    justice, 171–78; unacceptable, 72.
    See also community service
American Revolutionary War, 24, 25
analytical Marxism, 12

anarchism, 65, 210n26
antiracism, 25, 83, 97, 101
Aptheker, Bettina, 29, 30
Aquinas, Thomas, 3
Arbery, Ahmaud, 98, 101
arrest rates, 180
Attica prison uprising, 35, 40

bail, 28, 123–25, 139, 143–45
Bail Project, 143
belief systems. *See* ideologies
Benningfield, Sam, 71
Bentham, Jeremy, 3
Biehl, Amy, 178
black critical theory, 9–15
black feminist theory, 9
Black Liberation Army, 25, 35
black liberation movement, 25–26
Black Lives Matter, 97
black nationalism, 10, 23
Black Panther Party, 18, 25, 27, 34, 36
black people: alleged criminality of, 101–2,
    118–19, 200; alleged inferiority of,
    23, 102; attitudes of, toward police,
    156; conditions of contemporary,
    likened to slavery and colonialism,

black people (*continued*)
22–25; conditions of contemporary, likened to wartime, 35–36; incarceration rates among, 118–19, 200; institutional racism confronting, 107, 200; slavery's significance for identity, cultural, social, and economic factors concerning, 68–69, 81–82; stereotypes of, 101–2, 107, 200; as target of government oppression and violence, 24, 26–32, 38, 40–41, 155–57. *See also* ghettos

Black Power, 18

black radicalism: anti-government sentiments in, 18–19; author influenced by tradition of, 8, 12, 185; autobiographical narratives of, 20–25; Davis and, 10, 19, 66–67; freedom as goal of, 20; influential thinkers for, 10; key issues for, 10; origins of, 18; and prison abolition, 44; publicity for, from high-profile court cases, 31–32; sources of inspiration for, 22–23; strategies for promoting, 38–42; utopian elements in, 193–94; violent resistance advocated by, 19, 22, 24, 25, 43

Bland, Sandra, 144–45

Brown, John, 22

capitalism: Davis's critique of, 88–89, 104, 112, 191; homeostatic thesis applied to, 110; just society compatible with, 126; liberalism distinct from, 11; manifest and latent functions of, 88–89, 108; Marx's critique of, 81, 83–84, 185–86; opposition to, 25;

oppression/injustice produced by, 125–26, 136; prison industrial complex linked to, 120–22, 125–37; racist foundation of, 104; social conditions under, 112; welfare-state, 12, 173

Charlestown State Prison, Massachusetts, 45–46

Cherry Hill prison riot, 46

Chesimard, JoAnne Deborah. *See* Shakur, Assata

Civil Rights movement, 67

coercion: justifications of, 60–62, 70, 129, 139–40; opposition to, 52, 65–66, 88; of prison labor, 73; in sentencing options, 72

Cohen, G. A., 12, 212n5

Collins, Ella, 46

colonialism, 22–25

community accountability, 171–72

Community Justice Exchange, 143

community service, 53, 54–55, 71–72, 74, 77, 116, 171

corrective justice, 85, 118, 199

corruption, in prison industry, 130–31

courthouse revolt, 28–29

courts. *See* judicial system

crime: black people stereotypically linked to, 101–2, 118–19; gender and, 164–65; hierarchy of, 53, 115, 157; justifiable, 60–61; policies on arrests for, 157; prison abolition not an abolition of, 101–2; protection of the vulnerable from, 55, 61–62, 85, 114, 115, 139, 165, 167, 170, 177, 183, 201; psychology of, 160–61, 193–94; rates of, 151, 200; reality of, 179–81; rejection of language and concepts

operating rights, 127
oppression: of black people, 26–32;
of black resistance/liberation, 38,
40–41; capitalism as source of, 125–26,
136; crimes attributable to, 60, 63;
dehumanizing/incapacitating effects
of, 63; of ghetto denizens, 26, 37;
police as source of, 26–28; prisons
as instrument of, 112–13; racism as,
89, 118; social illusions fortifying, 97;
U.S. government as source of, 19, 24,
26–33, 35–42; of the vulnerable, 114
outsourcing, 127, 140, 142
ownership rights, 127

pacifism, 66
penitentiary, 48–49
perverse incentives, 133–35
philosophy, 3, 13–14
Plato, 3
pluralism, 14
police: abolition of, 156; effectiveness of
deploying, 154–57; reform of, 157–58;
violence used by, 26–28, 101, 155–58,
176
police-court-prison apparatus. See law
enforcement
political activism, 13
political prisoners: autobiographical
narratives of, 20–25, 35, 37–43; black
radicals as, 19–25; ghetto denizens
as, 35–38; idea of, 19–20, 32–34; as
prisoners of war, 36; resistance
strategies of, 38–42; resulting from
prisons' basic societal function,
89–90; Soledad Brothers as, 28, 31
poverty abolition, 191

pretrial detention, 48, 122–25, 139, 143
prevention of crime: effectiveness
of imprisonment for, 52, 54,
148–49, 151–52; as justification for
imprisonment, 52–54, 61, 129; mental-
health care and, 167–68
prison abolition: antiracism and, 97;
basis of, 2, 6; black radicalism and,
44; crime downplayed in arguments
for, 179; Davis and, 5–8, 19, 37, 44–45,
48–49, 66–67, 168, 183–84, 189–90,
204n15; diversity in movement for,
5; facilities that are target of, 49;
limitations of arguments for, 16, 66,
78–79, 81–84, 86, 102–3, 107–12, 183,
195–200; models for, 20, 22; need for
social-structural reform as upshot
of arguments for, 16, 86, 111, 117, 138,
146–47, 195–201; and non-reformist
reforms, 17; pacifist justification for,
66; prison industrial complex as
target of, 120–21, 146; prison reform
vs., 2, 6–8, 17, 46–49, 51, 59, 69, 76, 79,
88, 91, 103, 112, 117, 152, 166–71, 186–90,
198, 203n4, 212n6; psychiatric hospitals
included in arguments for, 210n20;
punishments acceptable from standpoint of, 54; school or workplace
abolition compared to, 102; utopian
character of, 15, 190–94
prisoners: decarceration of, 116; families
of, 2, 75–77, 131, 139, 149, 186; freedoms of, 77–78, 170; public attitude
toward, 131, 134, 159; public costs of
maintenance of, 74–75, 210n19;
reentry and reintegration of, 159–60,
170; reforms for improving lives and

DISCUSSION QUESTIONS

1. Prisons have often been studied from historical and social-scientific perspectives. What can we learn from studying the practice of imprisonment from a *philosophical* point of view? What philosophical questions does prison abolition raise? What are the limits to a philosophical approach to this subject?

2. What does Shelby see as the fundamental disagreement between prison reformers and prison abolitionists? In what ways does Shelby say abolitionists are opposed to reform efforts in prison systems in the United States and elsewhere?

3. Shelby focuses closely on the life and writings of the scholar-activist Angela Davis. Do you think this focus was appropriate given the aims of the book? How are the "revolutionary prison narratives" from the Black Power era similar to classic slave narratives during the antebellum period? How are they different?

4. What are the legitimate aims of imprisonment, according to Shelby? Do you regard these aims as legitimate, and if

so, under what conditions? Are there aims of imprisonment that Shelby or Davis rejects or ignores that you see as legitimate?

5. How does Shelby respond to the charge that prisons are inherently dehumanizing? Is it feasible to eliminate the dehumanizing aspects of many existing prisons? What, if anything, might give us confidence or hope that such changes are possible?

6. What are Shelby's main objections to the analogy between slavery and imprisonment? What, according to Shelby, are the limits of the genealogical critique of prisons as "a legacy of slavery"? Do you find these criticisms convincing? Why or why not?

7. Are racism and prisons inextricably linked in U.S. society such that only the abolition of prisons can effectively break the link? Does Shelby offer convincing reasons for thinking the link can be broken without ending the practice of imprisonment?

8. What is the "prison industrial complex"? Can one consistently oppose the prison industrial complex without being a prison abolitionist? Can we separate opposition to the prison industrial complex from opposition to capitalism itself, as Shelby suggests?

9. Shelby believes that prisons can, and sometimes do, help prevent or control crime. How, according to him, do they do so? Do you find his arguments persuasive?

10. Shelby welcomes and even embraces many of the alternatives to prison that abolitionists propose: enhancements to mental health care, drug-use disorder treatment, noncarceral rehabilitation services, restorative justice measures, community-based mutual aid, and so on. However, he is doubtful that these alternatives are sufficient to maintain a reasonable level of public safety in a modern society and so thinks that prisons are socially necessary. What are his grounds for taking this position? What, for him, are the limits of non-carceral methods?

11. Abolitionists are often dismissed as utopian dreamers. Shelby thinks that there are good dimensions to abolitionist utopianism. What are these? What are the bad aspects of this utopianism that he describes, and do you agree that they are bad?

12. Shelby agrees with abolitionists that dramatic structural transformation is called for in the United States and that such social change would greatly reduce the need for prisons. He ends *The Idea of Prison Abolition* by calling for the abolition of *ghettos*—metropolitan black neighborhoods that suffer from concentrated disadvantage and mass incarceration—rather than the abolition of prisons. Do you agree that this is a call that radical reformers and prison abolitionists, despite their other disagreements, can and should share?